# Revolutions of Our Time

# Social

John Vaizey

# Democracy

Weidenfeld and Nicolson   5 Winsley Street   London W 1

© 1971 by John Vaizey
Printed in Germany by Mohndruck Reinh. Mohn OHG, Gütersloh
Designed by David Eldred for
George Weidenfeld and Nicolson Ltd, 5 Winsley Street, W.1.
Picture research by Josephine Labanyi
ISBN 0 297 00261 9

# Acknowledgements

The pictures in this book are reproduced by the kind permission
of the following:
ANSA, Rome: 183 *lower picture;* Arbejderbevaegelsens Bibliotek,
Copenhagen, 144–5; Arbeterörelsens Arkiv, 143; Archiv für Kunst
und Geschichte, 49, 51; Archiv Gerstenberg, Frankfurt, 139; Atelier
Populaire/Dobson Books, 199; Auckland Collection, 155, 196; Bi-
bliothèque Nationale, Paris, 26–7, 28; BBC, 176; British Museum,
10 *top left and right,* 36 *bottom and centre,* 38, 53, 69, 84, 89
*below,* 90, 96, 97, 103, 105, 116, 187; Camera Press, 156, 195 *right,*
205; Chicago Tribune, 140; The Communist Party of Great
Britain, 33; Conservative Party, 161, 180, 217; Cortauld Institute,
36 *top;* Cummings/Daily Express, 212; Deutsche Fototek, Dresden, 102; Friedrich Ebert Stiftung, 44–5; John Freeman and Co,
10 *top right,* 36 *centre,* 84, 96, 103, 105, 116; Kathy Henderson, 91;
Indian High Commission, 195; Institute of Slavonic Studies, 172;
International Magazine Service, 181; Jak/Evening Standard, 213;
Jensen/Sunday Telegraph, 215; Keystone Press Agency, 136–7,
138, 186; Labour Party, 62, 121, 160, 185, 203; London School of
Economics, 123; Jan Lukas, 167; Meridiane, Bukarest/Jasmine
Spencer, 12 *above;* Moro Rome: 10 *lower picture,* 12 *lower picture,*
98, 99, 100, 101; Musée de Strasbourg, 32; New Lanark Associa-
tion, 21 *lower picture;* Novosti Press Agency, 80–1, 82–3; Paul
Popper, 114–5, 151, 169, 173, 175; Radio Times Hulton Picture
Library, 8, 21 *upper picture,* 22–3, 31, 64, 65, 68, 71, 73, 74–5, 79,
118–9, 124, 128, 129, 130, 146, 148, 183 *upper picture;* Gordon
Robertson, 10 *top left,* 36 *bottom,* 38, 53, 69, 89 *lower picture,* 90,
97, 187; Scarfe/Private Eye, 204; Snark International, *title page,* 56,
106, 111, 112, 134, 150; Staatsbibliothek, Berlin, 95 *left,* 95 *centre;*
Süddeutscher Verlag, 43, 89 *upper picture,* 92–3, 110, 214; Syn-
dication International, 163; T. U. C.: 17, 24, 55, 78; U. S. I. S.,
London, 208; Vicky/Evening Standard, 190, 200, 206; Victoria and
Albert Museum, *endpaper,* 57, 95 *right,* 126; Whitelaw/Daily
Herald, 159; Derrick Witty, *endpaper,* 57, 95 *right,* 123, 126, 161,
180, 185; Zentral Bibliothek, Zürich, 41.

# Contents

For A.G.W. affectionately

# SOCIALISM!

# Introduction

Socialism has to be defined more by what it is not than by what it is. On the one side stands liberal capitalism, with its distrust of the state and its emphasis on competition and the liberation of the individual from many (if not all) social principles of obligation. On the other side stands communism, with its totalitarian identification of the individual with the state and its identification of liberty with the realisation by the individual of a collective social purpose. Socialists have sought to tread the middle way. In the Second World War English socialists like J. B. Priestley defined England's future as a country embracing the best of American capitalism and Russian communism (both allies of the British at that time); and throughout the 1930s and 1940s Sweden was held up as the example of a country which, while aiming at equality and prosperity by social intervention, managed to give its people the greatest degree of individual aberration from the mean. Legalised abortion on the welfare state seemed to be the symbol of an ideal socialist society, and was contrasted with the suppression of the Kulaks in the Soviet Union on the one hand and mass unemployment in America on the other.

Socialism, then, is best defined as a self-conscious middle way. Its original doctrine was opposition to capitalism, its later doctrine opposition to communism. But for many years communism and socialism were synonymous; after Marx they were regarded, by some, as separate successive historical stages, but the socialist movement was not yet split cleanly from communism. The split came when Bernstein and other thinkers differed from the majority of Marxists on the nature of revolution and the direction of the bourgeois state. For Bernstein, as for the Fabians, the state was a mechanism for social improvement and for the gradual achievement of socialism; for the Bolsheviks it was an instrument of the bourgeoisie, with no possibility of other use. After the Bolshevik seizure of power in Russia the

## What is Social Democracy?

**Opposite:** Unionist poster from the British general election of 1924. Socialism, in the person of Ramsay Macdonald, straddles the gulf between decent capitalism in search of new Empire markets and Soviet communism. The Bolsheviks are shown as devils incarnate surrounded by flames

*Right: The capitalist in action:* cartoon from Keir Hardie's *Labour Leader* during the miners' strike of 1894. *Far right: The socialist answer:* 'Tomorrow.' The Miner: 'Your right, brother capitalist? ... your are entitled to a lamp and a pick ... like the rest of us.'

Popular socialist postcard from Italy. Such idealised (and usually female) figures, wearing flowing drapery and carrying torches or trumpets appear in the graphics of many countries and embody that utopian aspect of socialism which offered hope for an escape from the realities of life

division between socialists and communists attained an objective basis. Political and economic actions by the Soviet government showed clearly that the Bolsheviks were not liberals, were not gradualists, and that they were apostles of violent revolution throughout the world. Socialists were parliamentarians.

Thereafter, socialism represented as much a response to communism as an alternative to capitalism. Whenever communism moved, socialism felt bound to move too, usually in a different direction. Socialism had become, by the late nineteenth century, part of the ordinary party system of liberal (and increasingly democratic) politics; socialist tactics and strategy were dictated more and more by the needs of the political situation in liberal countries; but socialist philosophy, when it came to take stock of where socialism was going, felt obliged to orient itself to the Soviet state. Because what was going on in the Soviet Union bore little if any direct relevance to the party politics of liberal states, socialist philosophy and socialist practice increasingly diverged.

It is difficult, therefore, to relate socialist practice directly to socialist philosophy, or to relate either to political and economic reality, since socialist practice has for the greater part been dictated by short-term parliamentary considerations, and socialist philosophy has been like the shadows on Plato's cave, reflected and refracted from capitalist societies to communism, and back to socialism, and then hastily related to what socialist parties were doing. To attempt to make socialist policies and principles consistent is self-evidently an impossible task, for both philosophical response and political urgency have led to innumerable accretions of policy and philosophy which are often incompatible one with another. But that is not unusual, for the same criticism could be made *mutatis mutandis* of liberal, communist, capitalist and catholic apologias. Yet, one doubts whether the criticism of incoherence when laid at the door of communist doctrine would have much force, for – doctrine or not – communism in its various forms manifestly exists, and though its forms vary, they have many essential features in common. It is a matter for dispute whether socialism exists in the sense that communism does, and certainly, if it does exist, then the regimes that have called themselves or are called socialist have little indeed in common.

How, then, is socialism to be defined? It is, first of all, parliamentary in conception and in operation. In the dispute between capitalism and communism, the socialists accepted the parliamentary political structure which the communists denounced as irredeemably bourgeois. Socialists put Parliament at the centre of their political institutions. This was an inevitable consequence of their decision to achieve socialism by gaining a majority in existing parliamentary institutions. It meant that socialists were organised in parliamentary parties, and that 'after the achievement of socialism', the party system would continue. This was in direct contrast to the communist view that in a socialist society parties would cease to exist since the development of a classless society would remove the basis for political parties. The acceptance of parliamentary institutions as the central feature of a political system marked, therefore, a clear break with Marxist principles and practice. This is the essence of what is meant, in this book, by Social Democracy: and if the traditional shorthand 'socialism' is often used, the contrast with other 'socialist' systems (whether Marxist or National Socialist) must never be forgotten.

Parliament, then, was at the centre, and socialists were one party among others. As a party they put themselves on the left, in an continental semicircular chamber ranged between the communists on *their* left, and the radicals on their right. Socialists, therefore, defined themselves as on the left of the parliamentary system; whenever the centre moved to the left the socialists moved left as well, to preserve their original

position. Thus, within the parliamentary system, the socialists were bound always to provide from their own members the most extreme of the parliamentary opposition (though, of course, there were extremists of the left and the right who were outside the parliamentary system); and at any particular time their orientation was bound to be part of the total orientation of the parliamentary system to the society in which it was functioning.

Their situation on the left meant that they were bound to choose the more populist course, and the more 'democratic' course, when choices were presented. The extension of the suffrage, first to all males, then to all adults, the extention of the right to elect officers and representatives in many institutions – all this conception of radical democracy, 'one man one vote', equal constituencies, and the secret ballot – were taken over from the Chartists in England and, ultimately, from the American and French revolutionary doctrines. The socialists developed the conception of representative democracy along the most liberal lines in all the countries where they were active.

In contrast to the liberals, however, their concern for democracy was accompanied by a different view of the role of the state. Under liberal capitalism the state was, ultimately, a referee; the game was played by the capitalists. According to the communists the state was an corrupt referee: it rigged the match against the proletariat. According to the socialists, the increasing majority of voters would be working class, and they would use the power of the state in their own interests. The nineteenth-century state, according to the Webbs and to later historians not of their persuasion, was a tremendous social invention, enabling the community to perform tasks that previously could not be performed at all. This was the case first of all in the social services, where education, health and social security could be provided free or cheaply with impressive consequences for the happiness and well-being of mankind, and secondly in the ownership and control of productive enterprises.

Thus, in practice, socialism came to mean the growing extension of state power through the public ownership of industry and the extension of social services.

**Opposite. Above:** Rumanian cartoon of the confrontation between workers and capitalist. *On the left*, non-organised workers. *In the centre*, social democrats. *On the right*, the communist party shows the strength of the united working class to bring about change by violent revolution. To the communists the social democrats had aquiesced in the capitalist status quo and lost all hope of effective action by supporting gradual reform through parliamentary action. **Below:** though taking up a reformist position the social democrats also had to defend themselves against right-wing accusations of communism. This Italian poster shows the problem merely by the amount of lettering it has to carry in order to make its position clear: 'Social democracy proves itself with reforms and well being. Communism proves itself with tanks. PSU Democratic Socialism: to the left but towards liberty'

Bismarck's social security legislation was copied in Australia, and then in Britain, with socialist advocacy. The state railway enterprises of the continent formed the forerunners of extensive public holdings in business and commerce, ranging from agricultural credit corporations in Scandinavia to coal-mines in Britain, and to airlines throughout the world.

The extension of state power was a further argument for public control. The analysis of capitalism's defects that underlay socialist policies laid stress upon the apparent fact that capitalism could produce goods but not sell them. The division between the owners of property, on the one hand, and the propertyless workers was seen as the cause of inequality of incomes, and an inequality that, in Marxist terms, would lead to the breakdown of capitalism because of the crisis of overproduction in which what was produced could not be consumed because of the absence of purchasing power. Thus socialism was intended to be a mechanism to boost purchasing power.

It was to do so by a redistribution of incomes away from the rich towards the poor. Under communism this would have been achieved by a general political convulsion in which the propertied would have been hanged from the nearest lamp-post, while their property was socialised. Under socialism the expropriation would be gradual: increasingly, society's surplus value would accrue directly to the state, and through progressive taxation the rich would be deprived of income which would be given to the poor. The rich, who saved, would be replaced by the poor, who would spend. This spending would also effect another change: production would now be of things made for use, rather than of vain fripperies made for the rich and sold for profit. 'Production for use and not for profit' was a slogan that carried with it many implications. One was derived from the utilitarian theory that extra goods gave greater satisfaction to those who were poor than to those who were rich. Another was that profit was a disreputable surplus derived from the exploitation of the poor, producing unnecessary goods for the wealthy.

The practical consequences of this view of profit were many. Inevitably egalitarian anti-profit measures were bound to commend themselves to socialists but the consequences for production and output were grave, for it turned out that capitalism had not solved the problem of production. This was seen most obviously in poor countries like India where a socialist government's most pressing problem was not distribution but output, but it was also seen in the third and fourth Labour governments in Britain (1945–51, 1964 –70) which were elected on egalitarian expenditure programmes but were forced to deal almost entirely with problems of production.

The difficulties of production were intrinsic to all societies, and a mistake had been made in believing that technical advance had gone so far that it would be possible easily and painlessly to incorporate it into physical capital and allow the production of abundance to proceed. The conditions for technical progress were complex, but they depended, certainly, upon the rapid and continuous accumulation of capital, which implied that a high proportion of total potential output would not be available for consumption but would have to be invested. If the rich were deprived of their surplus, which they had largely saved and made available for investment, then the state would have to save. This made 'production for use' according to social priorities, (selling at or below cost) an unfeasible process for publicly owned industries. Increasingly, therefore, the debate about the ownership of property became a debate about how business was to be managed.

A publicly owned, democratically controlled economy is a concept that immediately raises the questions, who is to manage the enterprises and on what principles are they to be managed? For public ownership is not the same as public control; a series of socially owned enterprises operating on no common principle could be anarchic, and (in their various ways) despotic.

A variety of answers were given. The first, historically, was that workers should control their own enterprises and run them by consensus, or by majority rule. This co-operative conception, as applied to whole enterprises, was called syndicalism. It was a French conception, applied first in the 1848 Revolution, and later in small ways elsewhere, culminating in experiments in Yugoslavia in the 1950s and 1960s. It had many drawbacks, but two stood out. Managerial skill is rare; and an enterprise needs managerial skill and authority to be exercised if it is to survive. This is difficult if not impossible in the given conditions. Above all, even if this difficulty could be overcome, there was no general rule by which the output and pricing policies of each enterprise were to be determined. It was implicitly assumed that the economy would function 'normally' as it did under capitalism.

At the other extreme from workers' control was state control. A municipal tramway in Belgium, a state electricity company in Latin America, the state coal industry in Britain, could all be managed exactly as though they were privately owned corporations. Except that profits went to the state (or the losses were borne by the taxpayer) there was no difference that could be discerned, immediately. Thus, the management of state enterprises was a perennial topic of discussion. At one extreme, syndicalism came near to the fascist doctrine of corporatism, in which the state consisted of groups of people organised according to their working groups; at the other extreme, state control came near to the conception of the all-powerful state, which libertarian socialists had set out to oppose.

The problem of workers' control arose not only because socialism had a concern for public ownership. It arose too because socialists called themselves a working-class party. In fact, at most times, a majority of the working class, and especially working-class women, voted for right-wing parties, and in many countries – France, Italy, Germany – a majority of those voting for left-wing parties voted communist. The socialists called themselves a working-class party for three reasons. It was their view that political parties represented different social groups – peasant parties represented the peasants, liberal parties represented the manufacturers and conservative parties represented the big landowners – and that they were the representatives of the working class. This sprang from their Marx-like interpretation of politics as a manifestation of the class struggle. In fact, the basis of party allegiance was far more complex than this simple-minded division would have suggested. The second reason for the socialist identification with the working class was the objective fact that in some countries they were the representatives of that part of the working class organised in trade unions (which was usually though not always a minority of the manual workers). Thirdly, socialists were a working-class party by aspiration, in the sense that they desired to redistribute wealth, income and power to the working class. It was this aspect of socialist thought that led to the great preoccupation with equality, and the notion that liberal equality in political terms was virtually meaningless without an economic and social interpretation as well.

But equality with whom? Socialists were from the start internationalists, in the sense that they were opposed to war, which they thought to be an aspect of capitalist competition, and they were positively in favour of supra-national institutions. But they were also nationalists – any small racial, ethnic or linguistic group was sure of their support in its demands for independence. Socialists were also unprepared to extend the concept of equality to equality between nations in any but a legislative, political sense.

This book begins with the theorists, who laid the foundations for what was to follow when socialist parties came to power. It surveys the activities and problems of those parties when power was attained, together with trends and developments which were materially to influence the role of socialist thought and action. The rise of socialist theory, its compromise with practice, and its final collapse into a pragmatic justification for nationalist scientific-militarism, is our theme. It is also the culmination of liberal theory and of a world-view that has dominated the west for centuries, though it is a nineteenth- and twentieth-century phenomenon. The rise of socialism is indissolubly linked with the rise of 'a science of society'; and the development of socialist theory and practice is symbiotically linked to the development of the social sciences. Any narrative and critique of socialist history is therefore, in some ways, a critique of the social sciences. But socialism is also a philosophy – a view of the world – which happens to be that of many, perhaps most, civilised people, including the author and his publisher.

International solidarity of labour was seen by the socialists as the only way to overcome the power of capitalism. But despite the international character of socialist thought the working classes rallied to their national causes in two world wars

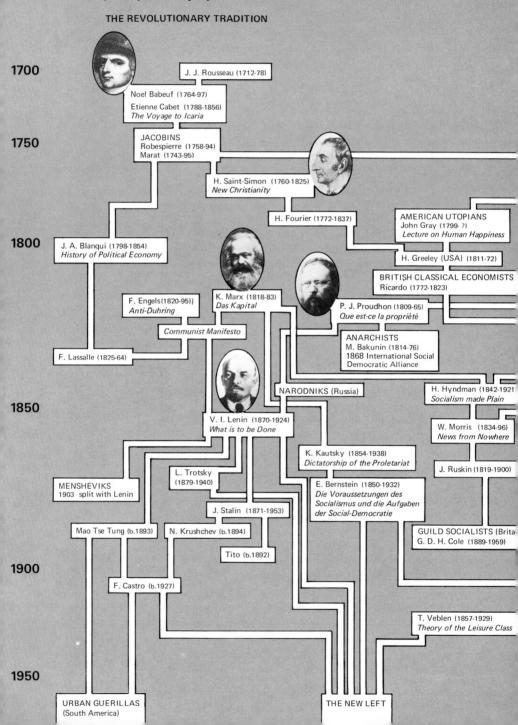

# Landmarks of socialism: indicating the relation of social democracy to the worldwide development of socialist thought and utopian philosophy

THE REVOLUTIONARY TRADITION

**1700**

J. J. Rousseau (1712-78)

Noel Babeuf (1764-97)

Etienne Cabet (1788-1856)
*The Voyage to Icaria*

**1750**

JACOBINS
Robespierre (1758-94)
Marat (1743-95)

H. Saint-Simon (1760-1825)
*New Christianity*

H. Fourier (1772-1837)

AMERICAN UTOPIANS
John Gray (1799- ?)
*Lecture on Human Happiness*

**1800**

J. A. Blanqui (1798-1854)
*History of Political Economy*

H. Greeley (USA) (1811-72)

BRITISH CLASSICAL ECONOMISTS
Ricardo (1772-1823)

K. Marx (1818-83)
*Das Kapital*

F. Engels (1820-95))
*Anti-Dühring*

P. J. Proudhon (1809-65)
*Que est-ce la propriété*

*Communist Manifesto*

ANARCHISTS
M. Bakunin (1814-76)
1868 International Social
Democratic Alliance

F. Lassalle (1825-64)

NARODNIKS (Russia)

H. Hyndman (1842-1921)
*Socialism made Plain*

**1850**

V. I. Lenin (1870-1924)
*What is to be Done*

W. Morris (1834-96)
*News from Nowhere*

K. Kautsky (1854-1938)
*Dictatorship of the Proletariat*

J. Ruskin (1819-1900)

L. Trotsky
(1879-1940)

E. Bernstein (1850-1932)
*Die Voraussetzungen des
Socialismus und die Aufgaben
der Social-Democratie*

MENSHEVIKS
1903 split with Lenin

J. Stalin (1871-1953)

Mao Tse Tung (b.1893)

N. Krushchev (b.1894)

GUILD SOCIALISTS (Brita
G. D. H. Cole (1889-1959)

Tito (b.1892)

**1900**

F. Castro (b.1927)

T. Veblen (1857-1929)
*Theory of the Leisure Class*

**1950**

URBAN GUERILLAS
(South America)

THE NEW LEFT

# THE UTOPIAN TRADITION

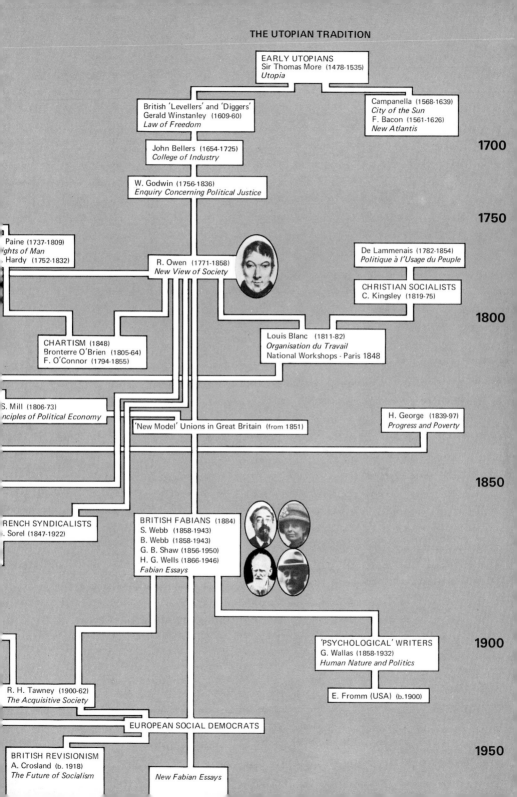

**EARLY UTOPIANS**
Sir Thomas More (1478-1535)
*Utopia*

Campanella (1568-1639)
*City of the Sun*
F. Bacon (1561-1626)
*New Atlantis*

British 'Levellers' and 'Diggers'
Gerald Winstanley (1609-60)
*Law of Freedom*

**1700**

John Bellers (1654-1725)
*College of Industry*

W. Godwin (1756-1836)
*Enquiry Concerning Political Justice*

**1750**

Paine (1737-1809)
*ights of Man*
Hardy (1752-1832)

R. Owen (1771-1858)
*New View of Society*

De Lammenais (1782-1854)
*Politique à l'Usage du Peuple*

**CHRISTIAN SOCIALISTS**
C. Kingsley (1819-75)

**1800**

CHARTISM (1848)
Bronterre O'Brien (1805-64)
F. O'Connor (1794-1855)

Louis Blanc (1811-82)
*Organisation du Travail*
National Workshops - Paris 1848

S. Mill (1806-73)
*nciples of Political Economy*

'New Model' Unions in Great Britain (from 1851)

H. George (1839-97)
*Progress and Poverty*

**1850**

RENCH SYNDICALISTS
Sorel (1847-1922)

**BRITISH FABIANS** (1884)
S. Webb (1858-1943)
B. Webb (1858-1943)
G. B. Shaw (1856-1950)
H. G. Wells (1866-1946)
*Fabian Essays*

'PSYCHOLOGICAL' WRITERS
G. Wallas (1858-1932)
*Human Nature and Politics*

**1900**

R. H. Tawney (1900-62)
*The Acquisitive Society*

E. Fromm (USA) (b.1900)

EUROPEAN SOCIAL DEMOCRATS

**1950**

BRITISH REVISIONISM
A. Crosland (b. 1918)
*The Future of Socialism*

*New Fabian Essays*

# Social Democracy before Marx

**Robert Owen**

It is possible to trace socialist thought back to Plato, to More's *Utopia*, to the Peasants' Revolt, to the Levellers in the English Civil War, but to do so is more to make myth than to trace a realistic line of descent. Robert Owen is the first genuine socialist because he was coincident with the industrial revolution and his concern was with the proletariat. Moreover he was involved in three movements which, in direct line, led to socialism: trade unions, co-operative societies, and welfare systems.

Robert Owen was a Welshman who worked in Scotland. Born in 1771, he bought the New Lanark cotton mills near Glasgow in 1800, and as a capitalist entrepreneur, ran them profitably, while paying good wages and establishing a miniature 'welfare state' with education for the children, medical care, housing, and welfare benefits. This side of Owen was paternalist and not specifically socialist, but it marked a radical departure from the traditions of laissez-faire capitalism. More significant was his foundation of the first serious trade union in Britain, and his followers' foundation of the Rochdale Co-operative Society.

These two events, together with his benevolence as an employer, were incidents in early industrialism. The nature of industrial capitalism was revealed first of all in Britain. It required high savings, a labour force prepared to work for money under conditions of industrial discipline, a continuous stream of technological innovations, ever wider markets, and a modern system of government.

In this context, with a population explosion continually adding to the ranks of the landless poor, the

Cartoon of Robert Owen's plan for a 'labour exchange' where, 'the poor may do without the rich, combine to supply each other with the necessaries of life, live in perfect equality and have leisure to improve their minds.' For most people however merely to suggest that men should be valued according to what they produce was enough to make the whole idea ridiculous

working class played a passive role. In times of unrest they provided the mob; in times of war they provided the soldiers and sailors; at all times they provided the labour force for the factories and workshops, and servants for the homes which belonged to the more prosperous classes.

Radical thinkers – Godwin, Saint-Simon, Fourier – argued for the incorporation of all men into the political society, occasionally adding to this some conceptions of social and economic equality. But much of their thought (which was, of course, extremely unsystematic) was coloured by the view that a return to an idyllic pre-industrial society was possible, on the basis of peasant smallholdings. Many socialists started or took part in rural settlements, somewhat like Israeli kibbutzim, and the redistribution of land, so that men could provide for their own needs and do without mass industry, was a continuing strand in populist and socialist thought. America provided for European radicals a continuing vision of free land that could yield

abundance; and a democratic society could only be
built, it was thought, in such a manner.

This vision provided a leit-motif for socialist thought
throughout the nineteenth century. Owen came to
share it, backing New Harmony in Indiana in 1824, and
establishing a settlement (on the site of an older one)
which was to teach the world how to live according to
new and better principles. American space, and the
sense of beginning anew, combined with romanticism
to suggest that a reformed society could be willed into
being by a spread of new attitudes. This view (which
came to be called Utopian) owed a great deal to religious revivalism and was not specifically socialist. What
was socialist was the analysis of the ills of industrialism,
as being due to the private ownership of capital, and the
diagnosis of social and personal conflict as springing
from the economic basis of industrial society. New
Harmony departed rapidly from these principles and
Owen, tired of the colony, left it to his younger sons.

He returned to England and found that the trade

unions, newly legalised, were organising the workers to protest collectively against social and industrial conditions. Owen then set out to realise his vision of the collectivist society through the militant working class, abandoning the paternalism of New Lanark and the private community of New Harmony. He did so first by seeking to establish producers' co-operatives which, trading with each other, would bypass industrial capitalism. These schemes, which rapidly spread, developed into a broader concept of a General Labour Union, and in 1834, after an earlier Owenite scheme for a Grand National Moral Union of the Productive Classes, there was founded the Grand National Consolidated Trades Union. The earlier Owenite scheme was for a general strike to bring capitalism peacefully to an end and to replace it by a co-operative commonwealth; the Trade Union was planned, by the same means, to achieve the more limited end of an eight-hour day of work. Owen still hoped for a common agreement by all classes to replace capitalism while the trade unionists, by class action, sought to modify it. And this was to be a recurrent socialist dilemma; they stood for goodwill among all right-minded men which they thought would inevitably bring about socialism, since socialism was the only reasonable society, but this action had to be for limited objectives by class-warfare techniques.

One of Robert Owen's 'Labour Notes'. These were an attempt to replace the established monetary system by making the currency represent directly the number of hours worked. Workers in co-operative institutions could exchange these for goods at co-operative shops linked with the National Equitable Labour Exchange

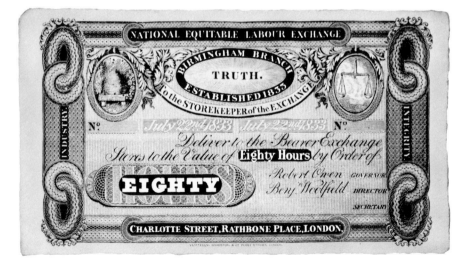

The Union collapsed: its aims were ambitious, its organisation feeble and its support evanescent. All that survived of Owen's schemes was the co-operative movement – an organisation of consumers that bought goods wholesale, retailed them to its members at prevailing prices, and distributed the profits to consumers in proportion to their purchases. Owen had challenged capitalism on four fronts: its industrial organisation, by a visionary community, through a trades union movement, and through a consumers' organisation. Out of three if not all four of these the socialist movement was to be constructed and the socialist challenge to industrialism mounted.

## Proudhon, Saint-Simon and Fourier

Proudhon (1809–65) was a Frenchman of working-class family, from Besançon. More than any other man he dominated French socialism, and because of Marx's denunciation of him he became the central figure in non-Marxist socialist thinking. He was not a system builder, a Utopian. He was, rather, a libertarian, almost an anarchist, devoted to 'liberty' and 'justice'. He was profoundly hostile to the state, which he thought of as essentially a repressive agency, and an enthusiast for law, which he regarded as an abstract entity embodying justice. The state, however democratic it might become, would inevitably revert to repression. The law, once established in fairness and justice, would stand unalterable and above society. The practical work of life would be carried on by groups or associations based on the family. Proudhon had an organic view of society: he deeply distrusted the co-operative societies, or companies, or free communities, that Owen had been concerned with, and which Blanc and Fourier, his predecessors in French socialist thought, had advocated. The family, according to Proudhon, would be able to work out its own salvation alongside other families working for the same end. Conflicting interests would be reconciled partly by a change of heart, since bad behaviour was a result of capitalism, but also by a process of combat. Proudhon had a vivid sense of opposites and conflict; an unnatural harmony, a supremely smooth-running system would have seemed to him a wicked nonsense. The incentives to work and to

*Drelin-din-din! Drelin-din-din! din!! don!!! din-don! din-don!!... puf! peu... l'instant, c'est le moment, profitez-en, ces farces ne dureront pas longtems........*

'The ideas fair.' Cartoon by Bertall from *Le Journal Pour Rire* of the various brands of socialist thought available in France in 1848. Represented as fairground charlatans are, from right to left: Victor Considérant and the followers of Fourier; Proudhon; Louis Blanc; Pierre Leroux with George Sand and the Journalist Thoré; a fictitious highwayman, Robert Macaire; and, in the foreground on the left, Etienne Cabet. The word 'socialist' embraced many political and intellectual positions, and was characterised by a great deal of hot air

improve one's lot were the supreme virtues of the family, and the recognition of the contradictions and difficulties inherent in society as a result of the struggles of separate families lay at the heart of Proudhon's view of the good society.

In this respect Proudhon represented a radical break with the French tradition. In the French Revolution Babeuf and his followers had argued for an egalitarian commonwealth, following the Jacobin denunciation of inequality and the disloyal attitude of the rich to the revolution. They had argued for communal property, operated by directly elected committees paid the same wages as the workers. Work was to be compulsory and only workers could vote. This state was to be achieved by a revolutionary dictatorship of the proletariat. Babeuf was executed for conspiracy to overthrow the regime, but his views remained underground, and sprang to the surface after the Revolution of 1830, which brought the bourgeois Louis-Philippe to the throne.

The title-page of a Saint-Simonian hymn. Saint-Simon maintained that production is the goal of human society. His followers, led by Enfantin, set out to spread his ideas and established a quasi-religious fraternity which eventually retired from the world to set up a miniature model of the perfect society at Menilmontant. The author of this commemorative hymn, Felicien David, was Enfantin's most faithful disciple

Saint-Simon and Charles Fourier took a less revolutionary line. Saint-Simon (1760–1825) was an aristocrat, who enlarged his future by speculation during the Revolution. He fought for the American revolutionaries and supported progressive causes. He sought to make a major intellectual contribution along the lines of the Encyclopaedists and his ambition was to found a universal science of mankind which would embrace all existing sciences and enable mankind collectively to plan its own future. To Saint-Simon, therefore, may be traced the socialist preoccupation with the social sciences, and their preoccupation, in turn, with universality, a tradition which Marx inherited (though rejecting its religious and visionary overtones). Proudhon was a pragmatic realist, preferring the known organic basis of social life – the family – to misty pseudo-scientific generalisations. Saint-Simon, out of his conception of universal history, foresaw the overthrow of the industrialist class by the workers; and the industrialists were (like Robert Owen) to operate their industries as trustees of the people. Here, again, Proudhon was profoundly opposed to Saint-Simon's paternalism. Included in this paternalism, in Proudhon's view, was the whole conception of planning the future of society and curtailing productive forces in the 'general interest' (a Rousseau-esque conception). The view that ultimately everybody would pull together in the same direction offended Proudhon's sense of the continual struggle in society.

Fourier, who was vastly opposed to Saint-Simon's vague and windy generalisations, came from a middle-class family (which was almost ruined by the Revolution) and, like Proudhon, from Besançon. He was not a Utopian, in the sense that he held that human nature was unchangeable and therefore could not be improved but he thought that, given the right social organisation, men could co-operate in ways which led to harmony rather than to strife. He regarded bourgeois society as a way of life which wasted men's time in trivial and worthless occupations – especially buying and selling – and he wanted them to eat splendid food, and drink good wine, which they themselves had grown in decent conditions. Like Morris and Ruskin he wanted to see honest craftsmanship the basis of a way of life, and

consequently he sought to establish communities where
people lived rewarding lives, following a diversity of
healthy jobs – growing food, weaving, carpentering –
and finding their chief enjoyment in honest work. He
envisaged a kind of kibbutz – a *phalanstère* (from the
Greek phalanx $\Phi\acute{\alpha}\lambda\alpha\gamma\xi$) – where families would have
their own rooms but where communal facilities would
be available. Incomes would not be equal but they
would be far less unequal than in existing society.

Fourier's ideas were practised in a few countries,
chiefly in North America, but his influence was profound, since he drew attention to the need to construct
a society which met the emotional needs of the individual, especially his need for happy and satisfying work.
It was in France, where society had never lost its peasant roots and where satisfaction of general needs was
not adequately achieved, that his ideas became firmly
rooted. Proudhon, certainly, though rejecting Fourier-
ism, by elevating the family to the centre of his
thought, emphasised precisely this aspect of full satisfaction of emotional needs. Proudhon argued that if
the credit system could be got right, so that the economy functioned automatically, an anarchic system
based on the family would be successful, and that such
a society would not only not be repressive, it would
be positively liberating of joy and satisfaction.

To Marx this was anathema. Initially he curried
favour with Proudhon, whose awareness of the complexity and contradictions of life was Hegelian he
claimed. When he found that Proudhon was unable to
help him, that he was not only not a Hegelian but was
opposed to abstract systems, Marx attacked him
violently. Proudhon believed there was no one way to
salvation; that, given freedom, especially freedom from
property (except purely personal possessions), because
'property is theft', the family structure could create a
diversity which would be part of the richness of living.
Marx, infuriated by this, developed his own ideas in
*The Poverty of Philosophy*, which was the basis of his
dialectical materialism. Proudhon may have been
unsympathetic, but his ideas were concerned with a
central question – how to make life, including work,
satisfying, and how to ensure diversity. Marx had
other goals in mind.

'The only way to destroy property.' Caricature of Proudhon who believed that the existing property relationships must be destroyed because they prevented the full development of human personality. A republic without a roof is suggested as an inevitable corollary of revolutionary violence

# Marx and the revisionist Marxists

**Marx**

Karl Marx was, in his personal life, one of the most disagreeable and distasteful great men of his time, much given to rage and anger, to intense self-pity, avid for praise, hostile to friends, allies, companions, constant only in deceit, and odiously vain. A Jew, he was a frenzied anti-semite; a scholar, his scatological abuse of rivals was pathological; a socialist, he despised the workers and hardly had a comrade in his life. His only

redeeming feature was his love for his elder daughter, Jenny. But he was a genius. His early work is obscure and almost unreadable; but with the *Communist Manifesto*, published in 1848, and *Capital* (of which the first volume was completed and published in his lifetime) Marx established two claims to fame. The first was a revolutionary, political vision of the overthrow of capitalism and its replacement by an egalitarian society, and the second was a view of the historical process which put capitalism and industrialism into perspective and suggested the mechanism by which it had come to power and the mechanism by which it would be overthrown.

Marx will not be understood unless it is realised that his own revolutionary influence was at most concerned with a tiny group – perhaps ultimately a thousand people in his own lifetime – of those entirely without power, with about as much immediate impact on nineteenth-century history as nudists or observers of flying saucers have had on the world since 1945. While the forces of industrialism swept the world, while revolution broke out all over Europe in 1848, and the French Commune came to power in 1871, Marx was on the periphery. His work was entirely theoretical, though

**Left:** One of a series of six woodcuts entitled *A New Dance of Death* by Alfred Rethel. These were produced in Dresden in 1849 and were immediately used as counter-revolutionary propaganda throughout Europe. Rethel sees revolution as a hollow trick played by Death. As a monstrous *agent provocateur* he enters a town and wins over the workers. He then distributes weapons, encourages fighting at the barricades (this picture) and finally rides triumphant out of the devastated city. **Below:** Manning the cobblestone barricades during the Paris Commune of 1871. This was a spontaneous rising by the Paris workers. To Marx it represented the prototype of the dictatorship of the proletariat by which a communist society would be achieved

he manoeuvred himself into office in the First International – the first revolutionary international socialist
movement – and destroyed it. Marx was the opposite
of Napoleon, who established a system of law and
thought as a result of practical revolution and conquest; Marx thought, and others subsequently practised. Moreover, in many respects, their practice was in
direct contradiction to Marx's own predictions and
recommendations. His texts were to be gone through,
as the Bible is gone through, for aphorisms and judgements that could be wrenched out of context and used
as justifications for what was being done.

The texture of Marx's thought was violent and
apocalyptic. He continually expected the downfall of
capitalism in the most violent revolution. He was extraordinarily authoritarian, both in personal affairs and
in his view of the world order. He expected the intole-
rant governments of Europe to be replaced by the dictatorship of the proletariat. (In fact the governments
were extremely tolerant and he operated with only
occasional brushes with the authorities, despite his
desperate attempts to overthrow them.) Thus, in inter-
preting Marxist doctrine, it must always be seen
through a prism of authoritarian violence.

According to Marx, the economy had progressed
from slave societies to feudalism, an agricultural
economy, and from there to capitalism. In each
society was to be found a class in control of the *new*
economic forces. In the case of feudalism this was the
capitalist bourgeoisie. It was their job to overthrow
feudalism and to endow humanity with industrial
capital. But to operate capitalism they had to have propertyless workers – the proletariat, from whose labour
the surplus was extracted to accumulate the capital.
But the proletariat, increasingly impoverished, would
be unable to purchase the goods that capitalism provided, and as a result, the machine would fall into crisis,
and – politically – the proletariat would rise. It would
overthrow the capitalist class with all its paraphernalia
of social and political machinery and thus under the
guidance of well-informed leaders the dictatorship of
the proletariat would be established.

There are two major points about Marx's thought
which are of supreme importance for the present

discussion. Firstly, how did he think capitalism worked and what were the main points of his diagnosis
which socialists could use for analysing (and attacking)
capitalism? The second is, what was his vision of
socialism and how did it differ from what democratic
socialists (as distinct from communists) would call
socialism?

Capitalism operated by the division of society into
two main classes who were at war – the capitalists and
the proletariat. The capitalists accumulated capital, by
buying and selling commodities at prices exceeding
their cost. Their profit represented the surplus value
over the wages paid to the workers. The value of goods
corresponded to the amount of socially useful labour
embodied in them; and the socially useful labour value
was determined by the objective technical considerations prevailing. The workers were increasing in number the whole time; as they competed for employment,
their pay tended continually to fall below subsistence
level. The fact that it did so meant that the entire
working class lived at (or just beyond) the verge of
starvation. The capitalists, seeking profit, would find
that, beyond a certain point, the rate of profit fell during
successive crises of overproduction, and they would
therefore seek overseas and colonial markets where
profit rates were higher. Colonial powers would go to
war with each other for markets (this was a view that
Lenin developed) and to this international chaos would
be added the internal chaos as the capitalists sought to
oppress and exploit the workers ever more intensively,
and as the workers sought to organise against the
capitalists. Capitalism was double-edged, so to speak.
Fighting against feudal societies, as in Russia, it was a
progressive force; fighting against the militant and
organised workers, it was a reactionary force.

The superstructure of the state reflected the underlying class relationships, which were deeply embedded
in economic reality. It followed, therefore, that the
role of the bourgois state was to aid the capitalists in
their exploitation; and that the notion of a state as
having regard to the welfare of its members, or of the
law being 'fair', was an idealistic fallacy.

The areas of dispute with Marx are obvious. First,
economics did not explain everything: – quite often

Marx's analysis of capitalism divided society into two principle and warring classes: the bourgeoisie **(above)** and the proletariat **(centre).** According to his scheme its survival depended on the continuing exploitation of the workers by the capitalists, a situation which would be brought to a violent end by the rising of the proletariat. This idea was basic to socialist thought as the cartoon **(below)** from Keir Hardie's *Labour Leader* of 1891 shows

socialists, on the other hand, rejected any form of dictatorship; they saw conflict surviving in a socialist society, and it was unclear as to what alienation exactly applied, for socialist societies were always unclear about the nature of authority in work, and the nature of payments for work, in an egalitarian society. Marx envisaged that under socialism the state would 'wither away' and a situation of gentle, cordial abundance would ensue, where non-perspiring peasants gathered the fruits of the earth with quiet dignity, as in some pre-Raphaelite painting. The harsh reality of Siberian prison-camps, show trials, and atomic spies was hardly a prelude to this roseate idyll.

But Marx's vision – both his dark vision of capitalism and his bright vision of socialism – dominated socialist thought. All socialist thought other than Marxist had to be defined in relationship to it. Two great German thinkers – Bernstein and Luxemburg – defined the non-Leninist socialist theory; while the English Fabians developed a line of reasoning which deviated increasingly from Marx. But both had major elements of Marx's thought incorporated in them.

The front page of the Danish newspaper *Social Demokraten* on the centenary of Marx's birth in 1918. Social democrats, although opting for gradual reform rather than violent revolution continued to recognise Marx's thought as the basis for theoretical analysis until well into the twentieth century. But as the implications of Soviet communism made themselves felt the social democrats rejected him completely in the attempt to differentiate themselves from the Bolsheviks

## Bernstein and German socialism

Edward Bernstein (1850–1932) was an important figure in German socialism, which was the most advanced in Europe in the late nineteenth century. Proscribed by the Anti-Socialist laws in Bismarck's Prussia, the Social Democratic Party had still, despite Bismarck, managed to get members elected to the Reichstag and to the various Landtags, even though party meetings were forbidden. By 1887 almost 10 per cent of German voters were voting Social Democrat and when the laws expired, in 1890, they polled 20 per cent. The parliamentary freedom of Germany enabled Members of Parliament to speak and vote freely, so that though the party was forbidden the right to engage in propaganda in the country, its Members of Parliament could argue on its behalf and fight elections. It seems, then, that the Anti-Socialist laws (like other oppression in pre-1917 Europe) were relatively mild by modern standards.

That being the case, it is apparent that by 1890 socialism had made little headway. In most big countries

## Percentage of Socialist/Social Democrat seats in the lower houses of the European parliaments between 1920 and 1970

| | 1920 | 1925 | 1930 | 1935 | 1939/40 | 1945/6 | 1950 | 1955 | 1960 | 1965 | 1970 |
|---|---|---|---|---|---|---|---|---|---|---|---|
| Austria | 39% | 40% | 42% | * | * | 45% | 43% | 43% | 46% | 46% | 48% |
| Belgium | 37% | 41% | 36% | 38% | 32% | 30% | 34% | 41% | 21% | 30% | 28 % |
| Denmark | 27% | 37% | 41% | 45% | 43% | 31% | 39% | 41% | 42% | 42% | 34% |
| Finland | 40% | 40% | 30% | 39% | 40% | 26% | 26% | 27% | 24% | 19% | 28% |
| France | 11% | 18% | 17% | 21% | 24% | 26% | 18% | 17% | 10% | 14% | 12% |
| Germany | 40% | 27% | 25% | * | * | * | 26% | 30% | 34% | 40% | 45% |
| Italy | 23% | 9% | * | * | * | 21% | 7% | 12% | 14% | 12% | 14% |
| Netherlands | 22% | 24% | 24% | 22% | 23% | 29% | 28% | 30% | 32% | 29% | 25% |
| Norway | 15% | 5% | 31% | 46% | 47% | 51% | 57% | 51% | 52% | 45% | 49% |
| Spain | 1% | 1% | * | 21% | * | * | * | * | * | * | * |
| Sweden | 34% | 46% | 39% | 45% | 58% | 58% | 47% | 48% | 49% | 48% | 54% |
| Switzerland | 22% | 25% | 26% | 26% | 24% | 21% | 25% | 25% | 26% | 27% | 25% |
| United Kingdom | 10% | 24% | 46% | 25% | 25% | 61% | 51% | 44% | 41% | 50% | 46% |

* = no free parliament

– Britain and the United States for example – it was not represented electorally at all. The socialist movement was a collection of small cliques with no effect on practical affairs. When the interminable wrangles of the Second International occurred, the disputes were about metaphysics rather than about practical realities. In France there were socialist deputies; but they were radicals rather than socialists, and in any case the French socialist tradition (based on Proudhon) was hardly recognised as socialist by the Marxists and post-Marxists. In a political sense, therefore, socialism hardly existed; far from being a spectre haunting Europe, as the *Communist Manifesto* put it, it was scarcely more than a bump in the night. For the bourgeois, socialists were but one of numerous minor groups of terrorists, assassins and trouble makers, usually living in exile. Among these groups of outcasts socialism steadily gained ground as an intellectual force, but only alongside other ideas – like that of nationalism – which in particular countries (Ireland or Hungary for example) were far more important. As it advanced, it added to itself disparate notions from these other groups. In Ireland, where nationalist feelings were strong after Parnell's organisation of the Irish Party, socialism had a strong nationalist context, as it did in India. Where they were weak, as in England, the ideas associated with socialism included pantheism, vegetarianism and the occult (all three embodied in the person of Mrs Annie Besant, the eccentric British theosophist). Thus socialism became a protean doctrine adding to itself other dissatisfactions with the world as it was. But it is important to remember that in the eyes of the world socialists were cranks.

The major step forward was to capture working-class institutions. As industrialism spread, there was a great growth of trade unions, co-operatives, working men's clubs, and other organisations whose membership was primarily or wholly working class. At no time in the nineteenth century did any of these organisations embody the whole of the working class: the trade union movement, especially, was based mainly on the more prosperous skilled artisans and barely touched the unskilled working class. The greater number of trade unionists and their leaders were conservative in religion,

Swiss cartoon of Kaiser Wilhelm battling with the manyheaded monster 'Social Democracy'. Despite his efforts the Social Democratic Party gained ground steadily. Its vote rose from 113,048 in 1871 to 4,250,329 in 1912

politics and ideas; but a growing group of younger members became socialists, atheists and advocates of other radical ideas. They too were often displaced intellectuals – self-educated men who fitted ill into existing society and therefore sought to change it. To them socialist doctrine offered an explanation of the alienation they felt and of the misery and unfairness they saw around them, and often suffered themselves, and the socialist movement, by offering a key role to the militant working class (that is, to them) offered them a practical and exciting way of changing things radically for the better. An alliance of socialist middle-class intellectuals and intellectual working-class trade unionists therefore offered a really effective possibility of action. The spread of universal male adult suffrage enabled this action to be channelled into parliamentary activity. The formation of working-class parties, like the German Social Democratic Party and the British Labour Representation Committee (the forerunner of the Labour Party) followed. Though they were working class in orientation, their leadership was often middle class and the greater part of the programme was drawn up by intellectuals, with special sops offered to individual working-class interests. Thus, though the socialists were to claim to be a working-class party, they were in fact an uneasy coalition of ambitious working-class leaders and middle-class people wishing to do good to the working class.

The German socialist dilemma was this. Proscribed by the Anti-Socialist laws, with only parliamentary activity possible, the socialists almost automatically classed themselves as a revolutionary party, determined to overthrow the Federal and the Prussian state and replace it with other political institutions. After its return to legality there was the possibility of achieving socialist aims within the constitution, provided that the Reichstag (for which universal manhood suffrage had existed since 1867) could achieve control over the executive, which was quite independent of the legislature and derived its authority from the Kaiser. The situation within the states themselves varied, but in general the legislative control of the executive was absent. Yet, should it be achieved, the socialists could combine with the liberals to out-vote the conservative parties.

Co-operation with the liberals had been anathema to Marx, and on most domestic issues the socialists and the liberals were poles apart – the latter believing in extreme laissez-faire and opposed to welfare measures – but on constitutional issues their positions were close. The socialist Gotha programme of 1875 envisaged such collaboration, and Marx had violently opposed it. Were socialists, then, opposed to the German constitution as such, and were they still a revolutionary party? If they were not, could they collaborate with the liberals? There was also the additional point, that the German Empire was militaristic; its first action, on its formation in 1870, was to wage war on France and annex Alsace-Lorraine; and the socialists were internationalists. If they attacked militarism, they attacked the Reich; and if they attacked the Reich, they were revolutionary.

The argument centred primarily on three figures; Liebknecht, Kautsky, and Bernstein. Liebknecht, a

Karl Liebknecht (second from the left) in the field in front of his quarters while on military service. He was murdered by the Free Corps on 15th January 1919 during the Spartacus uprising

Marxist follower, originally held firmly to the belief that the socialists were a revolutionary party; but by 1891, at the Erfurt Congress, he had so modified his position as to accept the possibility of successfully achieving socialism by parliamentary means. At this, the left-wing socialists promptly left the Social Democratic Party, which now embarked on a programme demanding parliamentary reform, (the secret ballot, biennial elections, women's suffrage) and the responsibility of the executive to the legislature and to the electorate. In the 1890s the great issue was whether or not to collaborate with the liberals to achieve social and industrial reform; and the liberals tacked about, at one time working with the socialists and at other times combining with other parties against them. By 1900 the socialists had finally decided that collaboration with the liberals was essential.

Kautsky, on the other hand, violently attacked the Social Democrats, in particular over their policy of coming to terms with the peasants and adopting an agricultural policy. According to Kautsky (and Marx) the peasants were not proletarians but reactionaries, and by aligning itself with them the Social Democratic Party abandoned socialism.

Kautsky, Marxist though he was, differed from

A group of delegates at the meeting of the Second International at Hamburg in May 1923. Eduard Bernstein is at the extreme right of the group

Lenin und Trotsky in that he thought socialism could
be introduced piecemeal and peacefully. But he did
believe that the growing centralisation of industrial
power which was apparent under capitalism would
continue under socialism and that it would entail a
highly-planned, centralised, socialist state. This was in
great contrast to the libertarian vision that informed
Proudhon and Owen and (in some moods) most other
socialists, even the Marxists; and it was a vision that
Bernstein adopted in his attack on Kautsky.

Bernstein was a 'revisionist' – that is to say, he said he
was a Marxist who, while accepting the central doctrine,
wanted to drop its politically unnecessary and offensive
irrelevancies. He wanted the Social Democratic Party
to be the party of immediate social reform – improving
labour conditions, removing taxes from goods largely
bought by the poor, regulating monopolies and trusts –
and the party which took the economy piecemeal into
public ownership. This implied that the state was not
necessarily an instrument of class oppression, and that
it was possible to use it for social transformation. For
Bernstein the vision of socialism achieved in its entirety
at one blow was Utopian. The way ahead lay through
detailed reforms, as Engels had argued in his last work.
(This was Bernstein's claim to be in the orthodox

Marxist tradition). Evolution rather than revolution was his watchword.

There is no doubt that Bernstein, in adopting an almost Fabian view of the possibilities of peaceful evolution, was radically breaking with continental traditions. He held that capitalism was not in the last stages of collapse; to German socialists this was heresy, for they believed in a catastrophic Day of Judgement. His reason for this break was philosophical, for he rejected historical determinism; inevitability had no place in a true social philosophy. Social and political forces could overcome economic forces. It was this assertion that marked a clear break with Marxist philosophy, properly understood, however much Bernstein might claim to the contrary. For socialism was not 'inevitable' now, its coming depended upon successful political action. And successful political action entailed the widespread acceptance, not of proletarian consciousness, but of a concept of the 'common interest', 'the public good', which would overcome individual and private interest and conflicts. Socialism must also be built on the achievements of liberalism and incorporate them within itself. 'It is true that the great liberal movement of modern times arose for the advantage of the capitalist bourgeoisie first of all, and the parties which assumed the names of liberals were, or became in due course, simple guardians of capitalism. Naturally, only opposition can reign between these parties and social democracy. But with respect to liberalism as a great historical movement, socialism is its legitimate heir, not only in chronological sequence, but also in its spiritual qualities...'. Having accepted, that is, liberal institutions, Bernstein went on to accept the German state. Socialists must be patient. They must accept the duties and rights of citizenship, including the responsibilities of the defence of their own countries. For Bernstein, therefore, social democracy was one party among others, – a socialist, democratic party of reform – but a party within the gradually improving social framework of the nation state.

The Party Congress rejected Bernstein. He was not expelled, however, because it was obvious that there was widespread support for his views. And, in practice, the party adopted his programme while retaining

Marx's theory. It was an odd position, and was shown to be such by the First World War and the revolution that followed it.

After 1900, the German Social Democratic Party was in an odd position. Despite the fact that the government was autocratic, in practice it found itself unable to govern without parliamentary assent; and if the Social Democrats allied themselves with other opposition parties they could out-vote the government supporters. But they were unable to ally themselves with these parties because to do so would imply assent to the basic principles of the regime, which they refused to give. They were poised, therefore, for inaction, so long as they had no independent parliamentary majority. To keep the party together, doctrine had to be kept pure. To get votes, the programme had to be heavily pragmatic and revisionist. In this way, the Social Democrats won more votes, and by 1912 they were the biggest opposition party, but still they could do little practical work, except by the size of their vote keep the pace for social reform quicker in Germany than in most other countries, as the other parties and the government sought to outbid them.

# Rosa Luxemburg

In understanding German social democracy it must be recalled that Germany's neighbour was Russia, a backward feudal tyranny of whose aggression all Germans were afraid, and therefore a strong army was a necessity; that Germany was in many respects a progressive and enlightened state, and that German socialists could assume that in many respects it was benevolently paternal; that southern Germany and east Prussia were backward and rural, while the Social Democrats were urban and sophisticated; and that Germany was autocratic and liberalism exceptionally weak. In such circumstances a successful Social Democratic Party was bound to be patriotic, autocratic, and given to making intermittent gestures of meaningless affection to the backward peasantry.

The international context in which socialism was developing had changed rapidly. When Marx disrupted the First International, socialists were a small group of people, chiefly refugees, at work in a few countries.

The Second International brought together growing socialist parties from many countries. As industrialism spread round the world, working-class organisations developed – trade unions, co-operative societies, political parties – all of which took on their own local colouring. These organisations all to a greater or lesser extent had a socialist tint; so that socialism became a generic term covering organisations and opinions from the palest pink to the deepest red. But it is important to understand that the split between communists – meaning Marxists – and the socialists – meaning Fabian, Bernstein-type revisionists – had not yet formally occurred. Though the socialist movement was continually splitting and regrouping, and people expelled each other from their ephemeral organisations with unfailing zest and regularity, it had a vague ideological unity in that its basis lay in Marx and Engels.

The world Marx had known was, however, gone. The international industrial system had been created; the proletariat was not immiserised; and the modern nation-state had been created. Western Europe and North America practically dominated the whole world. The peaceful atmosphere of the nineteenth century was breaking up and an arms race to accumulate modern weapons was accelerating. Socialism, politically speaking, embraced constitutional reformist parties like the Labour Party in Britain, the Social Democratic Party in Germany, and the Socialists in Scandinavia, on the one hand, and the revolutionary conspirators on the other hand. Among the industrial powers Russia was the only repressive autocracy; she alone, therefore, generated serious revolutionaries. The revolutionaries elsewhere, like Zapata in Mexico, were of the old-fashioned kind, though often they acquired a smattering of socialist jargon. Yet, while the Russians were virtually the only serious socialist conspirators (with practical experience in the Revolution of 1905), the German party, as well as most other continental parties, officially held to the revolutionary doctrine, derived from Marx, that in the crisis of capitalism they would take over the state, representing the intelligent, conscious vanguard of the working class. Apart from the Russian rising of 1905, the debate about revolution and its place in socialist thinking was highly

abstract and remote. In practice, though rejecting
Bernstein's revisionism, German social democracy was
revisionist. The British Labour Party, under Fabian
influence, was openly so. It seemed that revisionism
was the order of the day.

The First World War, the Russian Revolutions of
1917 and the revolutions in Germany, Hungary, Ireland and other countries, that accompanied and followed the Armistice of 11 November 1918, turned the
debate from an abstract one to reality; they turned
petty squabbles into life-and-death struggles; and they
finally achieved the split between Marxist communists
and social democrats.

It was Lenin who formalised Marxist revolutionary
doctrine, who was rushed to Russia after the first
revolution in 1917, who overthrew the liberal regime
of Kerensky and achieved a communist dictatorship in

Rosa Luxemburg
flanked by portraits of
Marx and Lassalle
speaking at a social-
ist meeting in 1907

Russia. With his collaborator Trotsky, who organised the Red Army, he overcame foreign intervention, won the Civil War, and established the dictatorship of the Communist Party – or of the proletariat – in Russia. Lenin played little part in the Second International, which was mainly a meeting place for socialists – meaning by that social democrats – who were seeking to play the parliamentary game to achieve power. Such a game could not be played in Russia. Lenin, therefore, embodied the Marxist tradition of a conspiratorial overthrow of an established regime, though the regime he overthrew was not capitalist but feudal. Lenin and Trotsky justified the establishment of communism in Russia by the expectation that there would be a general world revolution; it was an accident of chronology that it occurred first in Russia. For them the First World War was the long expected crisis of capitalism, while the German revolution which overthrew the Kaiser in November 1918 was the beginning of the capitalist collapse.

The theory of this collapse was developed by Rosa Luxemburg, a Polish Jew, born in 1870, who joined the revolutionary organisation 'Proletariat' at the age of sixteen. Poland, divided among the powers, was continually striving for nationhood, and Proletariat was organising the workers in Warsaw and other industrial towns against the Russians. In 1888 she fled to Switzerland, where she became a Marxist, and came to represent Polish socialists at the Socialist Congress of 1893. She moved to France, then became a German by marriage, and from 1900 onwards she worked in Germany. As a socialist theorist, Rosa Luxemburg was a major figure. First, in the growing identification of socialist and nationalist movements, she became a staunch internationalist. The international working class claimed deeper loyalty, it seemed to her, than fatherlands, and in view of the subsequent development of national socialism, this was of supreme importance. These views split the Polish socialists, most of whom were nationalists.

Secondly, out of the experience of the underground Polish movement, Luxemburg insisted that the Marxist policies, while seeking the dictatorship of the proletariat, should be democratic within themselves and in close touch with the masses. Lenin was strongly opposed to this: he believed in complete control of the party from the top, and this was always the practice in Russia after the revolution. Thus, had Luxemburg's views come to dominate the socialist movement, the communist development might have taken a different course.

Luxemburg's main claim to fame was her reinterpretation of Marx's laws of capitalist development. She

argued that capitalist development was spreading throughout the world, bringing the underdeveloped countries into its net, and that it was this continuous expansion that kept the rate of profit up and allowed wages to rise rather than fall. Obviously there was a limit, which would be achieved when there were no fresh lands to conquer. This thesis later seemed extremely apposite as an explanation of the great depression of 1929–34, when the so-called 'stagnation thesis' was widely held by economists, that the slump was due to a lack of profitable opportunities for investment. Luxemburg also argued that the struggle for markets and for opportunities for profitable investment would lead to wars. It was in these wars that she saw the opportunities for mass unrest, and for the Party to seize control. Thus, in her thinking, she was a revisionist as far as democracy went, but she rejected the relatively naïve optimism of the revisionists about the peaceful transition to socialism. Her theoretical work, too, on the economics of socialism was subsequently to be of great significance.

War broke out in August 1914. Despite passionate appeals, all socialist parties rallied to their national causes. Honourable men in all countries stuck to the internationalist line – Ramsay MacDonald in Britain, Luxemburg and Kautsky in Germany – and were repudiated. But the horrors of the war, the 1917 Revolution, and the squalor of the peace confirmed, it seemed, the Marxist diagnosis. In 1918 the Kaiser abdicated. A social democrat, Friedrich Ebert (1870–1925) became President of the Weimar Republic. In Berlin the revolutionary socialists rose in the Spartacus movement. It was overthrown, and in 1919 Luxemburg, a lifelong invalid, was murdered and her body thrown into a canal. In some ways she was the cleverest of the socialists, and her letters from prison suggest that she was also the most decent human being. Thereafter, social democrats lived out the tragedy of the Weimar Republic, to be succeeded by Hitler's National Socialist Party, while Lenin and Trotsky, and their successor Stalin, developed communism in Russia. Henceforth socialism was to mean something that was neither communism nor national socialism. The question was this: was Weimar's ineffectuality endemic in socialism?

'Joining the ends together again.' A rather optimistic prediction from 1914. With socialist parties everywhere abandoning the international solidarity of labour for their national causes in the First World War, the international network had indeed broken down

# Utilitarians, Pragmatists and Fabians

## The Fabian Society

British socialism had many strands. There was Robert Owen, with his co-operatives, his community, his paternalism and his trade union. In the 1850s and 1860s British trade unions organised the skilled workers; their leaders were of great respectability, and with the extension of the franchise to most urban males in 1867, some of the trade-union leaders became interested in parliamentary representation, an interest which was given a further fillip as the liberals and conservatives gradually began to encourage working-class participation in government, especially at local levels. Other working-class organisations also grew rapidly, especially the co-operatives. So an important strand in British socialism was a growing working-class experience in taking part in public life, and a wish to do so on an increasing scale.

The intellectual tone moved away from extreme laissez-faire as the nineteenth century progressed. There were some Christians who called themselves socialists and who thought that the message of the Church and of its Founder was strongly hostile to the ethics of capitalism. Christian socialists like F. D. Maurice were few, but they were the tip of an iceberg of moral disapproval of many aspects of capitalism and of industrialism.

There was an aesthetic revolt against industrialism which took the form of an interest in and a revival of medievalism – the revival of Gothic architecture, for

Membership certificate of the General Labourers Amalgamated Union. The extension of the unions from the craft workers to non-skilled workers came late and only gained real strength with the New Unionism of the 1890s, marking a movement towards more radical ideas

Woodcut by Walter Crane from *Cartoons for the Cause*. Crane's work is the most graphic example of the medieval revival undertaken by the Fabians in their revulsion against industrial capitalism

example, or William Morris's handcraft workshops – and a revival of the concept of an organic community, based on shared values and experience, to replace the cash nexus and the destructive competition of capitalism. This aesthetic revolt was of supreme importance. Nowhere had the impact of industrialism been more distasteful than in England – a small, beautifully landscaped island over which hideous urban sprawl, squalor and debasement had spread like a sore, until it had become unbearable to civilised and sensitive people. The tradition of wholesome craftsmanship had been broken, to be replaced by the endless repetitiveness of mechanisation. It is no exaggeration to say that in some – perhaps most – respects industrialism was a cultural disaster. The countries that best survived the disaster – Scandinavia, France and Italy – escaped early industrialism.

Of fundamental importance among the influences on British socialism was the impact of the Utilitarians and John Stuart Mill. The Utilitarians, inspired by the writings of Jeremy Bentham, believed that happiness could be quantified and that society should be based on the principle of 'the greatest happiness of the greatest number'. John Stuart Mill, with his deep-rooted concern for individual freedom, developed this doctrine in his own highly distinctive way. He too believed in the greatest happiness of the greatest number (he was – consistent with such a belief – a prominent feminist) but he was also concerned with the quality of that happiness. As a young man he went through a spiritual crisis, a sort of nervous breakdown, which was one of the most memorable illnesses in intellectual history. Reacting to his austere, rational upbringing, his emotions rebelled. He felt empty, hollow. If all his schemes for improving man's lot were carried out, would he be happy? The answer was that he would not. His reaction was important, for he did not abandon his radical ways and utilitarian thought, becoming a Roman Catholic or a Hindu. He kept to rational paths, but saw that, for him, true happiness consisted in altruism and the enjoyment of the creative arts. The creativity of the artist, that is, had a validity of its own. It was this deepening and strengthening

The handweaving looms in one of William Morris's handcraft workshops at Merton Abbey. Morris rejected the technical advances of the industrial revolution for their alienating and oppressive effect on the lives of the workers. He set up his handcraft workshops because he believed that life would only be good for all men when everything was shared and they worked for the joy of creative effort instead of selling themselves to an employer intent only on his profits

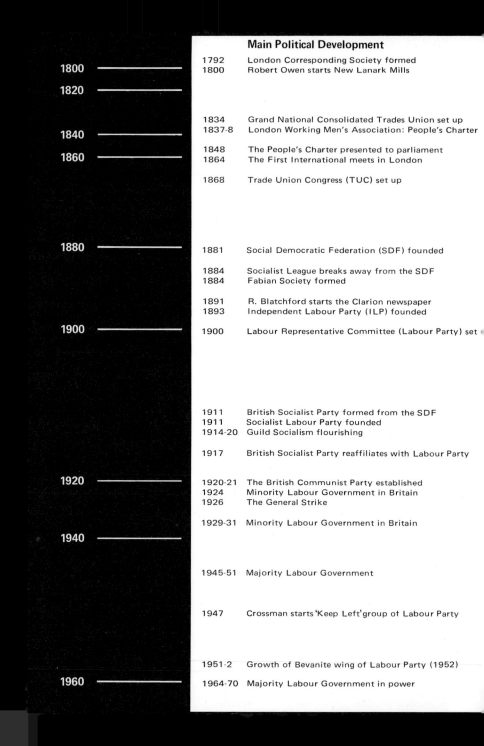

## Main Political Development

| | |
|---|---|
| 1800 | |
| 1820 | |

1792    London Corresponding Society formed
1800    Robert Owen starts New Lanark Mills

1834     Grand National Consolidated Trades Union set up
1837-8   London Working Men's Association: People's Charter

1848     The People's Charter presented to parliament
1864     The First International meets in London

1868     Trade Union Congress (TUC) set up

1881     Social Democratic Federation (SDF) founded

1884     Socialist League breaks away from the SDF
1884     Fabian Society formed

1891     R. Blatchford starts the Clarion newspaper
1893     Independent Labour Party (ILP) founded

1900     Labour Representative Committee (Labour Party) set

1911     British Socialist Party formed from the SDF
1911     Socialist Labour Party founded
1914-20   Guild Socialism flourishing

1917     British Socialist Party reaffiliates with Labour Party

1920-21   The British Communist Party established
1924     Minority Labour Government in Britain
1926     The General Strike

1929-31   Minority Labour Government in Britain

1945-51   Majority Labour Government

1947     Crossman starts 'Keep Left' group of Labour Party

1951-2   Growth of Bevanite wing of Labour Party (1952)
1964-70   Majority Labour Government in power

| | Social Change and Legislation | | Major Setbacks |
|---|---|---|---|
| | | 1819 | The Six Acts |
| 1824 | Repeal of the Combination Acts | | |
| 1832 | First Reform Act passed | | |
| 1833 | First effective Factory Act | | |
| | | 1834 | 'Tolpuddle Martyrs' transported |
| 1846 | Income Tax begins | | |
| 1867 | Second Reform Act | | |
| 1870 | Education compulsory to age of 10 | | |
| 1871 | Union funds safeguarded by law | | |
| 1872 | The Secret Ballot is instituted | | |
| 1874 | Two Miner's leaders become MPs | | |
| 1875 | Right to strike made legal | | |
| 1875 | First effective Public Health Act | | |
| 1883 | Corrupt elections made illegal | | |
| 1884 | Vote to all male householders | | |
| 1888 | London County Council is set up | | |
| 1894 | Death Duties, first graduated tax | | |
| | | 1901 | The Taff Vale Dispute |
| 1906 | Trades Disputes Act protects pickets and Union funds | | |
| 1908 | Childrens Act. First Old Age Pensions. | | |
| 1909 | Labour exchanges set up | 1909 | The Osborne Case |
| 1909 | Poor Law Commission Minority Report | | |
| 1909 | 'People's Budget' taxes the rich | | |
| 1911 | National Insurance established | | |
| 1911 | MPs paid for the first time | | |
| 1914 | 'Triple Alliance' of workers | | |
| 1914-18 | Government control of industry grows | | |
| 1918 | Universal Man and Mature Women Vote | 1918-21 | Government control of industry dismantled |
| | | 1927 | The Trade Disputes Act |
| 1928 | Vote to women between 21 and 30 | | |
| 1929 | Block Grants to Local Authorities | 1929-33 | The Depression |
| 1939-45 | Government economic control grows | | |
| 1941 | Free School Milk and meals for all | | |
| 1942 | Beveridge Report | | |
| 1944 | School leaving age raised to 15 | | |
| 1945 | Family Allowances | | |
| 1946 | New Towns Act passed | | |
| 1946 | Trade Disputes Act of 1927 repealed | | |
| 1946 | Electricity and Coal nationalised | | |
| 1948 | Nationalisation of the Railways | | |
| 1948 | Abolition of plural voting | | |
| 1948 | National Health Service set up | | |
| 1949 | Iron, Steel and Gas nationalised | | |
| | | 1953 | Steel is de-nationalised |
| 1965 | Re-nationalisation of Steel | | |
| | | 1971 | Industrial Relations Bill |

of his character that gave to his thought a characteristic note which was to become the hallmark of English socialism. Allied to detailed bureaucratic plans for social and industrial improvement, he expressed a concern for the organic life of the community and for its creativity that was entirely lacking in the advocates of laissez-faire and the Marxists. Mill, in his essays on Bentham and Coleridge, put his own position as a judicious mixture of the two, with a strong emotional leaning to Coleridge, but in fact, if anything, his instincts were to lead him in a socialist rather than a conservative direction. To make bureaucracy non-philistine was a characteristic hope of British socialists.

Thus 'socialism' in Britain was a mixture of Marxism, utilitarianism, Owenism, and utopianism, of Christianity, of trade unions, of aesthetic disgust with industrialism, and also (it being England) sheer eccentricity. The socialist movement was extremely small until the First World War. The original working-class Members of Parliament were working men elected with liberal support ('Lib-Labs'); it was only after the New Unionism of the 1890s had spread trade unionism to the unskilled workers that the working-class Members of Parliament, like Keir Hardie, became Labour members who were socialists. The characteristic English socialist doctrine was Fabianism.

The Fabian Society was founded in 1884 as an offshoot of the Fellowship of the New Life, whose very name suggests the cranky nature of the group. The Fabian Society's key members were Sidney and Beatrice Webb, Bernard Shaw and – for a while – H. G. Wells. Their doctrines were an amalgam of other doctrines, drawn partly from Ricardian economics, partly from John Stuart Mill, partly from Marx and partly from the accepted doctrines of liberal England.

The Fabians were first and foremost a constitutional, anti-revolutionary body. Their view was that the permeation of existing institutions and political parties at national and local levels with their ideas would speed up a process of change whose direction was in most respects inevitable. Capitalism was becoming larger and larger in scale, and more efficient in the process. As it did so, inevitably the municipalities – which provided an increasing range of services, from water to gas, from education to tramways – would take over the main work of production. A system of social security and medical care would eliminate poverty; a systematic programme of public investment would eliminate unemployment. Capitalism, in their view, suffered from lack of planning and from inefficiency. They adopted Ricardo's notion of rent, as a surplus over the costs of production paid to the landlord, and (following Marshall) applied it to all unearned income, including profit and interest. The income of the rentier was rent. If the ownership of property were collectivised, the rent could be used partly for collective purposes (education, parks etc.) and partly to reduce prices. Their main policies, therefore, were for the municipalisation of power, and its democratisation, which they regarded as an inevitable corollary of the ever increasing size of industrial units. The impracticality of this scheme was that the municipalities were quite unprepared to assume this role; and the Fabians only thought of it because the process of local government reform in England coincided with the early years of their activity, when some of them were serving on local government bodies. The municipalisation doctrine was replaced, subsequently, by the doctrine of nationalisation – partly because of continental experience (many continental railway systems were nationalised) and partly because of the obvious strength of the central government compared with the municipalities.

Politically the Fabians could be described as radical imperialists. In the South African war, when Britain went to war with the two small Boer republics, and British opinion was split, liberals and radicals supported the Boers, the Fabians supported imperialism. It was the function of advanced industrial countries to bring the benefits of industrialism and urban systems of government to benighted peoples. This view caused uproar. It seemed cynical, bureaucratic and technocratic. Ironically, three-quarters of a century later, in the case of Rhodesia, the left of the day took the Fabian line. Within this intellectual context of growing industrialism, the Fabians were radicals – they wanted to take up all social institutions by the roots, examine them, scrap them if they were weeds, and, if they were

Sidney and Beatrice Webb with Arthur Henderson at the time of the 1923 Labour Party Conference, of which Sidney Webb was chairman and Henderson the secretary. It was at this period that Sidney Webb coined the phrase 'the inevitability of gradualness' to sum up the Labour Party's philosophy

capable of growth, prune and replant them. Ultimately their philosophy became the dominant philosophy of the Labour Party, spreading to large numbers of people who would not have thought of themselves as socialists but as pragmatists.

What, then, did their philosophy consist of? It was a belief in the power of the social sciences to analyse social situations in great detail, to predict their future courses, and to suggest remedies and changes. In the Fabian view these sciences were neutral politically – economics was economics, sociology was sociology – but an honest examination of the evidence would convince people that socialism was not only inevitable but reasonable. The London School of Economics which the Webbs established was not a school for socialists propaganda – indeed most of its staff were never socialists – but the Webbs thought that by giving a boost to the study of the social sciences, a shift to socialist policy recommendations would be inevitable as social scientists were called in to examine social problems and suggest remedies.

Beatrice Webb's own experience on the Royal Commission on the Poor Laws confirmed this judgement. She was a well-born, rich daughter of a businessman called Potter, who took up social work and married beneath her class – a clerk of extraordinary ability and industry called Sidney Webb. Together they used her money to study social institutions – trade unions, co-operatives, local government – in great detail. When a Royal Commission on the Poor Laws was appointed Beatrice was made a member and undertook a series of massive investigations into the causes of poverty, and recommended, in a Minority Report, a series of major innovations in social administration – including a public health service, old age pensions, social security based on national taxation, public creation of employment, and a comprehensive range of local social services for the care of the sick, the disabled, the old, children and the unemployed, available as of right for all who needed them.

The Webbs, therefore, were pioneers of what came to be called 'the Welfare State', which comprised a comprehensive range of public social services and became a characteristic achievement of socialism. They recommended such measures as a result of what they called 'scientific' investigation of social phenomena. 'Scientific' was a word used not in a Marxist sense but in a bourgeois sense – that all men of good will, using the same techniques honestly, would reach the same conclusions on the basis of the same agreed evidence. The Fabians, therefore, appeared deluded to the Marxists who saw science, just as much as religion, as a manifestation of economic reality, and who considered that the function of bourgeois science was to rationalise – not to explain – the exploitation of the workers by the capitalist.

Allied to the Fabian belief in science was a strong, pragmatic approach to social and political institutions and problems. Pragmatism was a virtue much cherished by the British, though to continental observers it represented intellectual incoherence and muddle in practical affairs. In the socialist context it meant that, like Bernstein, the Fabians were prepared to achieve social reform by any (legal) means, even if it meant supporting conservatives against liberals, radicals, or even (on occasion) socialists. It also meant that for Fabians

Rupert Brooke, the poet, was a founder member with Hugh Dalton of the Cambridge Fabian Society. Many intelligent and sensitive people began at this time to think of themselves as socialists

the ideological issues were of far less importance than the building of bureaucratic machinery for social improvement.

The Fabians were bureaucrats. They believed that if the administrative arrangements were got right, all would be well. Most problems were matters of professional judgement, so that if it was made possible for people to give dispassionate professional judgments, the best would be achieved. Thus they wanted to ensure that doctors were free from financial pressures when they treated patients, and when they certified to the public authorities whether their patients were well or ill, and so qualified for benefit. The Webbs wanted teachers, engineers, housing officials to make social judgements in an atmosphere free from political pressure, or pressures to do anything other than what their professional judgement told them. This attitude was, of course, eminently reasonable; it appealed strongly to the rapidly growing class of professional people; and it was profoundly paternalist. The Webbs were, for example, deeply hostile to syndicalism and to anarchy.

The Fabian attitude to democracy was complex. On the one hand, they wished to subordinate almost all aspects of social life to elected representative bodies. The early agitation of the Fabians was concerned with suffrage and electoral reform. But the power of the elected representatives was in fact to be limited in two ways: first, the actual administration of affairs was to be by professionals, exercising (within a broad policy framework) their own independent professional judgement, and second, the elected representatives would share with each other and with their professional advisers certain basic assumptions about the way that the world should be governed. In the Fabian philosophy the world was without tensions, conflict or strife: a cool scientific approach would solve all problems.

It is an attractive view, very much in the utilitarian manner, but it is a curiously empty one. And it certainly bore little resemblance to the apocalyptic strife of the twentieth century. When Beatrice and Sidney Webb's ashes were deposited in Westminster Abbey, in the presence of a Labour Prime Minister, the social life of Britain was in large part their creation. But the world of wars, of revolutions and of deep dissension was far from their way of thought, and it may be that such a world that represented, ultimately, the reality that socialism was concerned with. That, at least, was the Marxist view.

The two major advocates of socialism in Britain (and, as a result, in the English-speaking world) were both writers – Shaw and Wells. Bernard Shaw (1856–1950) became the enemy of cant and the advocate of honest personal relationships, and he took an uncompromisingly radical line in sexual and moral matters. Nineteenth-century radicalism was largely concerned with two things – moral questions (including the truth or otherwise of Christianity) and the franchise. On the first of these – moral and personal issues – Shaw stood out as a friend and ally of any progressive cause that could be found. This is important for an understanding of the nature of socialism. Respectable nineteenth-century opinion imposed a code of accepted behaviour

## Shaw
## and the arts

George Bernard Shaw posing as a bust between Virgil and Homer at Bantry Bay, Ireland. Shaw was in many ways the 'jester' of the Fabian Society and certainly the most flamboyant of its leaders

which was formidable in the extent and rigidity of its tenets. Though many people broke the code they did so in secret, and when they were publicly discovered they were disgraced. Wilde was convicted of homosexuality and sentenced to imprisonment. Parnell was found to have committed adultery. He was destroyed as leader of the Irish Party. Even in libertarian France, President Faure's dramatic death, still embracing his mistress while *rigor mortis* set in, until her terrified screams brought assistance to release her, was hidden, and an official, all-male deathbed scene was drawn. To transgress the letter of the law was to invite disgrace, as George Eliot found when she lived respectably but 'in sin'. Yet to live by the spirit of the moral law – to love, to be true, to be frank, to be upright – brought no reward. It was to support the spirit of love, truth and freedom that the artists and moralists rose in revolt against the prevailing moral laws of the time.

It would be foolish to assert that the writers and painters were united in their revolt. As always, the majority probably shared the greater part of the thoughts and beliefs of their countrymen. But most of the active, creative spirits were critics of society. Zola in France, the Impressionists, Huysmans and Maeterlinck – all were united in what they opposed, through divided in what they supported. But the fact that, in Britain, two influential and extremely popular writers like Shaw and Wells were radicals and socialists was of great importance. It made it seem as though there was an organic link between the revulsion against nineteenth-century morality and socialism.

Shaw's was one of the most eloquent expressions of the revulsion. He championed Wagner and the new music. He was passionately in favour of Ibsen as the new social-realist dramatist, dealing with adultery, venereal disease and domestic tyranny rather than drawing-room comedy. He was a convinced aetheist. He was a feminist regarding the 'degradation' of women as a result of their propertylessness, and the exploitative relationships that were inevitable in a commercial society, so that marriage was a contract between unequals. (He himself married, well into middle-age, a millionairess.) He thundered about domestic tyranny, of youth over age. He was a vegetarian, an opponent of blood sports, an advocate of reformed spelling, a dress reformer – in fact, for every received opinion Shaw provided an alternative, generally one tending in the opposite direction. He put forward a new decalogue – including the aphorism 'Do not do unto others as you would be done by, their tastes may be different' – and, though people did not necessarily agree with him, they slowly ceased to hold the opinions that formerly prevailed.

His plays showed his opinions forcefully, and his prefaces related them to an analysis of capitalism which suggested that it was caused by inadvertance, and was inefficient rather than vicious. He showed respectable capitalists drawing their dividends from slum property; prostitution as an inevitable corollary of late marriage (postponed for property reasons); moral uplift as no substitute for social services; and class as mainly a matter of accent and attitude and not based on innate characteristics. The implications were clear. Capitalism made people hypocritical because it had to defend its inefficiencies by a mask of lies. Tear away the tissues of lies and the inefficiency would be exposed; expose the inefficiency and people would move voluntarily to a more rational society.

## H. G. Wells and science

As a writer H. G. Wells (1866–1946) had three characteristics, besides the facility and abundance that marks the successful and usually the distinguished author. He was a Utopian – greatly gifted in fantasy about the future. He was a realistic wry novelist about the comico-tragic failures of shopkeepers and small bourgeois. And he was, above all, a Scientist. Wells was trained as a scientist, and he greatly admired scientific achievement. His criticism of the world in which he grew up was that it ignored and despised science, rejecting the fact that it could – and would – transform the world, and man, and man's view of the world. The way that science would effect this transformation was through new social arrangements. Science applied to major problems required large-scale organisations, and that pointed to the nationalisation of industry. It implied, too, that power should be given to the technically qualified, not to gentlemen amateurs who happened to

be nominated by the private owners of capital who had inherited their authority.

Wells' fundamental belief in science and technology was the hallmark of a certain kind of socialism which became very influential. The impression was held by growing numbers of people that man's disinterested intelligence could unravel the secrets of the universe. The scientists were thought to be *ex hypothesi* disinterested; as they toiled away in their white coats they were the models of the New Men and the New Women – uninterested in wealth or ostentatious display, frank, open, comradely, interested in things for themselves rather than for their own glory. This idealisation of scientists was set against a picture of the typical muddled capitalist, his fingers continually in the till, spending his time obstructing the march of progress and looking down on the low-born but high-minded scientist. Remove the capitalist and his politician lackeys, organise government on a rational basis, create a world authority, and the power of science would be unleashed. Mankind would be ennobled by scientific education and fed, housed and clothed by the new technology. Whizzed from country to country, or from planet to planet, by nuclear energy, a new race would inherit the universe.

The obvious fallacies in this line of reasoning do not need to be pointed out: Wells recognised most of them himself early in the First World War. What does need to be emphasised is the attractiveness of the doctrine, and it was attractive because large parts of it were true. In all countries, among young intellectuals and semi-intellectuals, the victory of scientific rationalism was won. God did not exist. T. H. Huxley was right. Science was on its way to a completely rational understanding of the world and the way in which it functioned – both physically and socially. Rarely has the conviction that the physical and social sciences would transform the world been as strong as it was in the first ten years of the twentieth century. And it was this feeling that Wells captured.

Wells' world was miles away from Marxism and it was scientific in a sense that Marxism never was. It was a world dominated by social evolution, not by revolution. The great sweep of evolution, from the

microbe to the universe, made the class war seem an irrelevance. Convert people to science, he argued, and you convert them to socialism; 'make socialists and you will achieve socialism'. If mankind could see straight it would alter things. Wells was a practical-minded visionary and a great popular educator. Through his influence, especially on school teachers, whole generations of people gew up in Britain to whom socialism was the rational way to organise a modern society. Class conflict never accorded with their own experience of the world.

The socialist movement that Wells, Shaw and the Webbs helped to create was always small. Between 1900 and 1914 a growing number of Labour Members of Parliament were elected, but they remained a small group, far less important than the Irish Party, for example. Yet, despite this small band of parliamentarians, there were dramatic developments in the political and social world. The first was the election in 1906 of a large Liberal majority which remained in office until 1916, and in the coalition government until 1922. Almost immediately there was a series of clashes with the House of Lords, which drove the Liberal Party in a more radical direction but also made it seem ineffectual. People increasingly turned against the Liberals because they seemed unable to implement their radical ideas. On several issues – Irish nationalism, women's suffrage and defence – they seemed unable to put a foot right. Increasingly, to be radical on these sorts of issues was to be on the left to the Liberal Party.

The Liberals enacted a considerable amount of welfare legislation, yet once more they lagged behind the advance of ideas and continued, by failing to adopt Beatrice Webb's Minority Report on the Poor Laws, to be put in a posture of conservatism, despite Lloyd George's histrionics. Only on the issue of progressive taxation, when Lloyd George's budget was unconstitutionally and unprecedently rejected by the House of Lords, was the Liberal Party able to capture the left-wing imagination. Even there, everything was soon lost by the atmosphere of financial scandal that hovered over Lloyd George, and of philandering drunkenness that emanated from Asquith. When the Liberals finally blundered, almost totally unprepared, into the First

**VOTE FOR**

Home Rule.

Democratic Government.

Justice to Labour

No Monopoly.

No Landlordism

Temperance Reform.

Healthy Homes.

Fair Rents.

Eight-Hour Day.

Work for the Unemployed.

**KEIR HARDIE.**

World War, no reasonably intelligent radical could conceivably have any enthusiasm for them. The support of the militant working class had already been lost. Between 1900 and 1914 prices rose and real wages in some trades fell. Trade union militancy mounted. This drove more and more trade unionists into active membership of Labour organisations and to seek independent Labour (and socialist) representation in Parliament.

When war broke out, therefore, the Liberal Party had lost all respectability in radical eyes. When Lloyd George joined the Conservative dominated coalition as Prime Minister in 1916, he split the Liberal Party into the 'squiffies' (appropriately named after Asquith) and the Lloyd George-ites. The socialist movement was ready to replace the Liberal Party, not only as the working-man's party but as the party of the radical, thoughtful, 'new' people. But, first, it was gravely afflicted by the issue of pacifism and internationalism. Socialists held that war was a manifestation of the capitalist struggle for power, and that – as Marx put it – the working class had no country. The majority of

*Keir Hardie on an ILP election Poster in 1895. Hardie was one of the first working-class Members of Parliament becoming a Labour member in the 1890s. He founded the Independent Labour Party (ILP) in 1893 in an attempt to create a mass working-class party which was neither Marxist nor Liberal but which pursued a moderate constitutional policy*

French socialists had always indignantly repudiated internationalism if it involved a renunciation of patriotism, and on the outbreak of war it was shown that this was true of a majority of socialists in every country. Only exceptional spirits like Ramsay MacDonald stood out and, in standing out, they brought obloquy on the socialist movement. Public opinion throughout the world turned chauvinist and reactionary. Yet, when opinion swung back after the war was over, socialism reaped the benefit. Less than five years after the Peace Treaty, MacDonald was Socialist Prime Minister of the British Empire. The opportunity came to him, as it had come to Lloyd George, to betray his principles. Like Lloyd George, he did so, immediately.

## The Cambridge economists and Keynes

It may seem curious to regard the Cambridge economists, Marshall, Pigou, and Keynes, as key figures in the development of democratic socialism, yet the modification of laissez-faire and acceptance of a mixed-economy owe a great deal to their work. Moreover, with the abandonment of Marxism as an ideological basis for socialism, its claim to be based upon a 'scientific' analysis of society meant that it relied increasingly upon the social sciences for its understanding of the forces that were to transform capitalism into socialism. Since economics was the leading social science, and since socialism almost from its inception had held that changes in the economy were basic to all social change, it followed that it was the development of economics which was to exercise the most important influence on socialist thought and on socialist practice.

Of all the great schools of economics, Cambridge was to be the most influential. The Austrian economists were for the most part identified with a sophisticated defence of extreme liberalism, characterised by Von Mises and Hayek. The Marxist school degenerated, with few exceptions, into an apologia for Stalinism. Pareto provided an ideological content for fascism. Marshall, however, the true originator of the Cambridge school, carried on the utilitarian tradition of pragmatic solutions to social questions which he had got from Sidgwick, the Cambridge utilitarian, and his colleagues.

Alfred Marshall (1842–1924) regarded the economic system as a self-regulating process of tremendous complexity. But, being a man of infinite caution with considerable leanings towards 'socialism' (in the sense that he wished to take steps towards improving social welfare by public action), he never produced a theory of the economy which held that the economy could only work on laissez-faire principles, and on no others, nor did he ever produce a capitalist manifesto.

So blandly did he present his views that when Sidney Webb read the *Principles* (at a sitting) he said 'Nothing new'. Yet, in fact, an explanation of the economic system had been produced which was new, because it explained why the system worked reasonably well and why dramatic changes were unlikely to improve it, but which was completely compatible with a considerable degree of public ownership of industry, progressive taxation, and with a considerable extension of social welfare provision. Of course Marshall was concerned that the mainspring of economic progress – the willingness to invest and to take risks in order to achieve a higher income in the future – should not be broken, and in his view it was probably the case that this was the main justification for private ownership of capital as a means of achieving the accumulation

John Maynard Keynes in his study. Keynes's *General Theory* has probably been the greatest single influence on modern western economic policy

of capital. To this extent Marshall represented an intellectual assault on Marxism, whose economic analysis rested on Ricardo.

But Marshall's system (at least as it was widely interpreted, for Marshall's thought was so complex that he carefully covered most eventualities), was unacceptable on two counts. First, it seemed to offer a justification

Unemployed workers in June 1922. Until the advent of Keynes unemployment was regarded as an uncontrollable phenomenon which simply occurred and retreated according to the movement of the trade cycle.

for the existing distribution of income, by relating incomes to productive efforts, or to the rewards for savings, suggesting that a more egalitarian distribution could only be achieved by a steady improvement of the productive skills of the labour force and by the accumulation of savings on their part. This was quite unacceptable to socialist opinion, which saw the

existing extreme inequality as a major reason for abandoning capitalism and saw no reason why rapid change should not be brought about.

The second weakness of Marshall's thought was that it provided no general explanation of the periodic crises of unemployment that afflicted the capitalist world. Even those who accepted Marshall's view that the rate of economic progress in the nineteenth century had been, by historical standards, exceptionally rapid, were bound to admit (as he did himself) that the periods at which hundreds of thousands of men and women were thrown out of work, and they and their families reduced to destitution, were (to say the least) severe blemishes on the face of capitalism. And, as the twentieth century opened, the periodic crises became, as it were, permanent: a continual pool of unemployment was created. In Marx's system this was the reserve army of the unemployed whose function it was continually to bid down wage rates to subsistence level. But in fact wages were not beaten down to subsistence level. It looked as though a less sinister, more ordinary explanation of the phenomenon was necessary.

These two limitations of Marshall's work were tackled by his pupils Pigou and Keynes. Pigou's contribution to socialist thought was to develop a technique for assessing the differences between private and public benefits. First he developed Marshall's concept of the diminishing marginal utility of money – that, beyond a point, each additional unit of money yielded a diminishing amount of satisfaction – to give credence to the notion that money taken away from the rich and given to the poor would add to the sum total of satisfaction, since the money taken away from the rich would have a low marginal utility, while the money given to the poor would have a high marginal utility. This argument for progressive taxation (and ultimately for equal incomes), was based upon a series of post-utilitarian assumptions about the possibility of comparing dispositions towards happiness (and also upon some more technical considerations). But it represented a breakthrough because, henceforth, in the social sciences the onus was on the supporters of inequality to defend their position. When the findings of sociology (in the British tradition) were added to this economic reasoning, the weight of the social sciences was turned in the socialist direction.

Pigou's other ideas were equally important. One was his distinction between private costs and public costs, and private benefits and social benefits. A man could operate a noisome factory to his private profit, but the smell would add to his neighbours' costs by way of increased discomfort; and similarly a service – say a railway – could be provided at a private loss while yielding a public benefit. When Pigou also demonstrated that industries with large fixed equipment would usually make a loss under competitive conditions and competitive pricing policies, there was a cogent argument for nationalisation on technical economic grounds. Many socialists – Dalton, Gaitskell, Crosland – were to base most of their economic arguments for socialism on the reasoning developed by Pigou.

Keynes accepted the Marshall-Pigou scheme of reasoning. It is important to emphasise that this was a liberal view of the economy. None of the three was a socialist. But the arguments shifted radically from an acceptance and justification of laissez-faire as the proper way to organise an economy, to arguments in favour of predominantly private control of business on the pragmatic ground that, despite their shortcomings, businessmen were likely to make fewer mistakes than civil servants and politicians.

Except, that is, Keynes argued, in the management of the total level of demand in the economy. Keynes demonstrated that there was no reason to suppose that an economy would automatically adjust at a full-employment, non-inflationary level, and he showed how by suitable manipulation of demand it might be put at that level. The manipulation of the level of demand, in conjunction with the monetary authorities, was the principal economic function of government in normal circumstances.

The significance of Keynes was twofold. He was right in practice, for when governments began to try to achieve full employment by manipulating demand, it was seen to be possible to achieve and maintain full employment (though not to avoid rising prices). Thus he presented a practical case for government intervention

# The Daily Herald

No. 345. [Registered at the G.P.O. as a Newspaper.]    FRIDAY, MAY 23, 1913.    ONE HALFPENNY.

*INDUSTRIALISM—"Sentenced to Life."*

**Right:** 'Industrialism' sentenced to life!' Front page of the *Daily Herald* of May 23rd, 1913 **Far right:** National Government poster from the 1931 general election. Socialism and particularly Fabian socialism grew out of an aesthetic revulsion against industrial capitalism and its consequences. But having decided on a gradual and constitutional process of reform the parliamentary socialists were bound to try and maintain the standard of life of their working-class supporters which meant maintaining their jobs, and thus the very enslavement which socialist theory saw as the root of all evil

in the economy which had been lacking until then. Indeed, the majority of well-informed persons would have held that government intervention was more likely to cause unemployment rather than to cure it, by removing the incentives to private capitalists to invest, since more government activity meant higher taxation. Keynes now showed that the opposite was the case. The radical difference that this attitude to public expenditure made can be seen when the experience of the Labour government in Britain in 1929–31 is compared with Roosevelt's New Deal. The former failed to tackle unemployment as it had no practical or

theoretical reasons for positive action, while the latter increased employment (though without at first any theoretical justification). Above all, however, Keynes showed that the Marxist interpretation of capitalism was in many respects wrong. It was not inevitably in crisis. It did not inevitably immiserise the proletariat. On the contrary, given proper governmental procedures, it was compatible with steady economic improvement. And then, Keynes argued, the real questions could be raised: what was civilisation for? What did mankind want to do with itself? Socialism, ultimately, was to be about these questions.

# The revolutionary years

## Mensheviks and Bolsheviks

The supreme event in socialist history was the Russian Revolution of October 1917 which brought the Bolsheviks into power. Thereafter socialism was to be defined in terms of the split between it and communism, and though at times the two were drawn together, for the greater part of the years after 1917 the two movements were irrevocably opposed ideologically and practically. To the communists the socialists were capitalist lackeys. To the socialists the communists were unprincipled tyrants. In the process democratic socialism lost the greater part of its Marxist roots,

though it made periodic attempts to keep them alive. Its search for a set of principles is its chief intellectual endeavour.

In 1917 the socialists were in alliance, generally speaking, with their governments in Britain, France, Germany and Italy. In all countries a minority of the socialist movement was pacifist, a smaller minority revolutionary. The world was sick of war. Social conditions were deteriorating. The senseless slaughter of soldiers was terrible. Nowhere was it worse than in the Russia of the Tsars, where socialism was forbidden and hence conspiratorial.

The Russian socialist movement was split into several parts. On one wing were social democrats in the Russian Parliament. On the other were 'maximalists' or terrorists. In between were the Mensheviks and Bolsheviks. Certain key issues came up. One was whether to regard peasants as 'proletarian'. It was apparent that peasant support was essential for a successful revolution. The Bolsheviks, necessarily, were hostile to peasant proprietorship, though Lenin was prepared to regard the Kulaks as incipient capitalists

Troops guarding the headquarters of the Revolutionary uprising in Petrograd in October 1917. The winning over of the Petrograd garrison to the Bolshevik side was a turning point for the success of the revolution.

and the others as incipient workers. The Mensheviks were prepared to have a mass party of workers and peasants, which implied a major role for the peasants but Stalin and Lenin were united that the proletarians must have the leading role and that the Bolsheviks must lead the proletarians. Stalin also argued for permanent revolution – against the concept that once a liberal regime was established revolutionary activity would cease to continue. The Bolsheviks also argued that the way to consolidate the revolution was by establishing control of revolutionary bodies like the soviets of workers, peasants, and soldiers and sailors, of which the St Petersburg Soviet had been a model. It had been, under Trotsky, a kind of nucleus of a possible provisional government rather than a source of revolution itself; the idea was to allow the revolutionary situation to evolve, and to manoeuvre the soviets into the key points of control.

The Russian socialists, then, were divided before 1917 into three main groups, though there were many more small factions. One group wanted to collaborate

with the liberals, achieve the revolution, and then support the liberals until industrialisation had been carried on long enough to create the conditions in which socialists could win an election. The Mensheviks took this point of view, except that they would not have collaborated with the liberals after the revolution. The Bolsheviks, under Lenin's guidance, advocated support for the liberals in the bourgeois revolution, followed by a false period of collaboration, after which they would stab the liberals in the back and establish the dictatorship of the proletariat.

This was the course which was followed in 1917. There were two revolutions. The first brought the liberals to power under Kerensky. Lenin was rushed back to Russia by the Germans. He arrived in St Petersburg and brought the Bolsheviks to support the new regime. Then his party seized power in October (old calendar – November new style). Kerensky, his government undermined from within, had made the fatal mistake of not ending the war with Germany. The armed forces rose against their officers, public

A modern Soviet painting reconstructing the second congress of the Russian Social Democratic Labour Party in London addressed by Lenin. Painted by Y. E. Vinogradev (b. 1926). It was at this congress that the Menshevik Bolshevik split ocurred and the two separate groups were formed

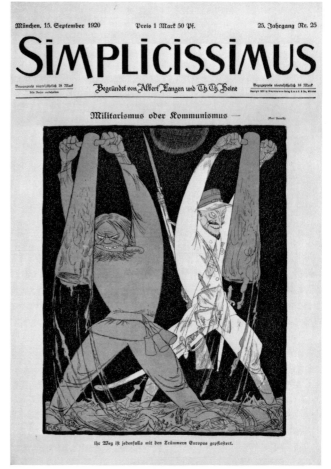

'Militarism or Communism. Either way their path is paved with the wreckage of Europe.' Cartoon from *Simplicissimus* in 1920. After the success of the October Revolution the Soviet Union suffered a bitter civil war and foreign invasion. There was no sign of an end to the bloodshed which had been going on since 1914 and it was hard to discern the emergence of the hoped for socialist utopia

order broke down, and the Bolsheviks seized power. They promptly inaugurated the second revolution by establishing the dictatorship of the proletariat, ending the war with Germany, and calling in the workers of the world to rise with them. In 1918 it looked for a while as though in Germany and Austria-Hungary this call would be listened to, and that the workers would rise, but in both Berlin and Budapest the risings were brutally repressed and no general revolt took place.

Lenin, Stalin and Trotsky, and their collaborators, found themselves in a strange situation. The first Russian Revolution of 1917 had overthrown absolutism, the second had overthrown the liberals. But it was not followed by world revolution. Instead Russia suffered from Civil War and foreign invasion until 1922. The dictatorship of the Bolshevik Party was established, but its establishment was accompanied by an almost complete collapse of civil order and of the economy. Paradoxically, Trotsky's organisation of the Red Army was the first triumph of the communist revolution; the other expected results obstinately refused to appear.

Lenin acted pragmatically, as had always been his way. The Bolsheviks organised a Third International (the Comintern) to work for world revolution and to organise support for the Russian Bolsheviks. Lenin also sought to establish some sort of relations with the bourgeois countries. Internally, he sought to conciliate the peasants. As the economic breakdown grew desperate, he restored a degree of capitalism to the agricultural system. When Stalin overthrew Trotsky, in the late 1920s, the capitalist experiment was drawn to a close and, with collectivisation, the conciliation of the peasants was ended. But up till the time of Lenin's death in 1924, and for some years subsequently, the Soviet Union was progressing, under the dicatorship of the proletariat, through a not wholly unconvincing parody of the capitalist stage of development.

Not since the heroic days of the French Revolution had the leaders of so great a nation sought so deliberately to reconstruct a society; and the Russian leaders were striving to do more than the French had attempted a hundred years before, because they were reconstructing the economy as well as the political structure of society. The impact of the Bolshevik Revolution was, inevitably, profound.

In the first place, it removed socialism from the status of a hypothetical fear that afflicted statesmen and businessmen in their cups, to an ever-present reality. The Russia of the Tsars had seemed ramshackle, but its very size and backwardness had seemed to give it a certain massive security. It was Russia, after all, that had brought Napoleon to his knees. Thus to normal conservative, constitutional people, Bolshevism became a very genuine threat; and all socialists were to be regarded, henceforth, as tarred with the same brush. The behaviour of the Bolsheviks, too, was repellent. Not only had the violence of the Revolution and the

Civil War been as repellent as violent revolutions and civil wars usually are, but the Bolsheviks had broken a great many of the more usual conventions governing the treatment of the defeated. Executions, expropriation and dispossession of the entire bourgeoisie on a massive scale seemed to be both their declared object and their actual practice. In addition, the Bolsheviks specialised in conspiracy and in deceit. They had plotted to achieve power and having got into office they had plotted and deceived their collaborators. They boasted of deceit. It was part of their plan. Whether in fact they were actually worse in this respect than any other group of politicans is a moot point; their honesty in admitting it was, of course, unforgivable.

Thus socialists who embraced liberal values were bound to be almost as horrified by the Bolsheviks as the capitalists were; and in addition they were to feel especially badly about the deceit and betrayal. On the other hand, by whatever mechanism and however bad the means, a socialist state was being created. Socialists were bound to admire this. And some of them were, perhaps inevitably, certainly understandably, to find excuses for what was done. Russia stood alone. It was surrounded by enemies. The communists had inherited an extremely backward economy and a tyrannical form of government. However illiberal the regime, at least the poor were being looked after. The long catalogue of excuses covered every evil, up to and beyond the millions who were executed and starved by Stalin's regime, and almost every socialist who denounced the Russian leaders for their evil ways felt in some degree guilty and disloyal for doing so. But the differences went back to the earliest foundations of communist policy by Marx, and its reformation by Lenin. Stalin was in their tradition. And democratic socialists had continually to recall that they were not. The difficulty of doing so was twofold: capitalism turned nasty, in Germany and Italy, and the non-Marxist socialists had only the weakest of doctrinal bases to oppose, on the one hand, capitalism and, on the other hand, Lenin and Stalin. It is the search for this doctrine, and the avoidance of the two extremes of opposing capitalism and fellow-travelling with communism that is the story of the thirty years after 1917.

The collapse of the German and Austro-Hungarian Empires, was less dramatic than the collapse of Tsarist Russia. The emperors of Germany and Austria went into exile and acceptable republics succeeded them, which were able (under protest) to sign the Versailles Treaty, giving Alsace and Lorraine to France and parts of Prussia to Poland. Austria and Hungary were separated; Czechoslovakia was created and given Austrian land with a substantial German-speaking minority. Trieste was given to Italy, and Yugoslavia was created by adding Montenegro and Croatia to Serbia. Thus the Balkanisation of Europe was a corollary of the dismemberment of Austria-Hungary.

**Germany**

Rosa Luxemburg and Karl Liebknecht had published *War and the Proletariat* in 1915; in it they advocated the continuation of the class struggle and just such a territorial settlement. When the war ended, therefore, it seemed as though in some respects the territorial settlement of Versailles was compatible with socialist aims. But these aims were to have been achieved by a rising of the international working class; they were in practice brought about by the collapse of the German economy, revolt in the army and the victory of the Allies. Meanwhile, the working-class revolution had taken place in Russia, over which Germany had first achieved victory, followed by the humiliating treaty of Brest-Litovsk, and against which the Allies were now sending an expeditionary force to help the counter-revolution. Thus, the risings of the German workers, though leading to peace, seemed to have led to a peace based on defeat. There had been strikes in April 1917, which had helped to bring the German economy down; in early 1918 they recurred; the Spartacists (the left-wing socialists) were behind them. The defeat occurred suddenly – a retreat in France, a government crisis in September 1918, the appointment of Prince Max of Baden as Chancellor on 3 October, a mutiny at Kiel, and a revolt throughout Germany. Thus it was the revolt which immediately preceded the armistice of 11 November 1918. Friedrich Ebert, the right-wing socialist leader, succeeded Prince Max on 7 November, Kurt Eisner formed a Socialist government in Bavaria. The Kaiser was deemed to have abdicated and he fled to Holland; abdication was forced through to forestall

Liebknecht's declaration of a soviet republic; Ebert wished to preserve the monarchy but the Republic was declared by Scheidemann in order to ensure a non-soviet republic.

The Republic was treated by the allies as the successor to the Kaiser: it was the Republic which accepted the armistice and signed the Treaty of Versailles. It was the Republic which guided the country through the horrors of the immediate postwar period, in which the Rhineland was occupied and the blockade was continued. Mass unemployment and great hunger were its immediate companions, defeat its midwife, and a savage peace treaty its immediate consequence. Ebert's government was formed from the socialist parties that had split earlier. Its job was to take over the regimes – both imperial and princely – which had collapsed. The socialists had three possible policies. First, to convoke a constituent assembly, which was the policy of the majority socialists; to establish a socialist republic, *de facto,* which was the independent socialist policy; and to establish a soviet republic, based on councils of workers and soldiers and sailors, which was the policy of the Spartacists. Ebert was a leader of the majority; Liebknecht and Luxemburg were leaders of the Spartacists. In the event, the majority opinion was accepted and elections were held.

The Spartacists had the precedent of the Bolsheviks for a second revolution to overthrow the first. But the German working class, which had flocked to join trade unions, was not revolutionary in this sense. The Spartacists, however, expected that the revolution proper – Marx's revolution – would occur in Germany, inevitably and rightly; and so they set out to make it. Without mass support they failed, hopelessly. They had some armed support, notably the Marine division, which occupied the Chancellery. On 24 December 1918 the army bombarded the Marines; but then a truce was arranged. The Spartacists declared themselves a communist party and sought to declare a soviet republic, occupying police headquarters in Berlin, and the office of the socialist newspaper *Vorwaerts.* Noske, the Minister of Defence, organised a Free Corps, or militia, which destroyed the revolutionaries, murdering Liebknecht and Luxemburg, and Luxemburg's lover, Jogiches.

**Opposite. Above:** A machine-gun being mounted on a lorry by Spartacists after taking over the guard position at Unter den Linden in Berlin. **Below:** Government troops on top of the Brandenburg Gate waiting for the Spartacists to attack. Two pictures from the fighting in Berlin in March 1919. By this time the unrest had spread throughout Germany, but, unlike Russia the social democrats managed to crush the revolt

Ebert with Noske, the Minister of Defence responsible for crushing the Spartakus uprising, bathing in a lake. The uprising and its defeat made irrevocable the split between the social democrats and the more extreme left. This split paved the way for the rise of Nazism in Germany by dividing the opposition to it.

In so doing, Ebert and Noske saved the democratic republic but they destroyed the left. The communists thus became the open and bitter opponents of the social democrats, and the Free Corps became a model for the Storm Troopers. The socialists lost the election of January 1919, though they were the largest party, with 11 1/2 million votes out of 30 million. A coalition was formed, of Democrats, the Catholic centre and the Social Democratic Party. In Bavaria Kurt Eisner, the moderate socialist Prime Minister, was assassinated. A soviet which tried to take over was dispersed, after a small bloodbath, followed by executions of well-known socialists. Thereafter Munich was a stronghold of the militant right. More fighting broke out in Berlin and over a thousand people were killed by the republican forces.

The Weimar consitution attempted to conciliate the left by giving workers representation in the directing bodies of enterprises and in joint economic councils at all levels. The works councils in factories were organised, but not those at governmental level, nor was the coal industry nationalised, as was expected. The situation was terrible; the blockade continued; starvation was widespread. Ebert's government had to sign the Versailles Treaty. Thus the Weimar Republic became the republic of traitors which Hitler was to overthrow thirteen years later. The Treaty was followed by a rising of the army against the government – the Kapp putsch – and the government fled to Stuttgart from Berlin. A general strike defeated the putsch. A new government was formed with a Catholic, Hermann Müller, as Chancellor. Kapp and his allies were pardoned, and the army, restored to its allegiance, was sent to arrest the members of the soviets set up during the strike. This led to the overthrow of the 'Red' Ruhr. Thus, by 1920, the socialists in government had an uneasy relationship with the army; because of proportional representation they were unlikely ever to get a parliamentary majority; they had alienated most of the active left; and they were detested by the patriots.

The troubles in the rest of Germany continued. Béla Kun, the Hungarian leader, arrived to organise revolt; he was sent by the Comintern. The risings occurred and were suppressed, and the communists lost much of their support. But they continued to take the view that a revolution was imminent. When, therefore, the communists sought to collaborate with the socialists, it was on the clear understanding that this was a temporary situation, waiting for the revolution. The social democrats were in a coalition with the Catholic Centre Party, and held office in some of the states. After more violence, including the murder of Walter Rathenau, a Law for the Protection of the Republic was enacted. The Comintern instructed the communists not to support demonstrations in defiance of the law but to concentrate on penetrating the trade unions. The Social Democrats, on the other hand, were committed to the Republic. It followed once more, therefore, that the Social Democrats were aligned with the bourgeois parties. A right-wing government followed, headed by Wilhelm Cuno. The government was unable and unwilling to disarm – if only because of fears of violent revolution. It therefore followed that they broke the disarmament clauses of the Treaty of Versailles. The French occupied the Ruhr. Inflation followed the government's payment of subsidies to the workers who indulged in passive resistance to the French. The collapse of the mark ruined the smaller middle-class and bigger working-class groups. Thus, by the end of 1923, the communists and the right were united in

A red five thousand mark postage stamp overprinted with the figure 2 million in black in order to keep pace with the inflation. These stamps ran into tens of millions of marks

regarding the Weimar Republic with profound distaste. The right – with its Free Corps and Black Reichswehr – was more para-military; the left was more conspiratorial. Though the Social Democrats detested Cuno's government, they were bound to defend the Republic; and as the attacks on it mounted they were put in an impossibile situation. In ten years Germany had fallen from the most powerful nation in Europe to ruin and the Social Democrats had always been on the 'wrong' side. It was a situation fraught with tragedy and irony, which developed an inevitability of horror upon horror.

After Cuno fell, the Social Democrats entered the Stresemann coalition, to restore the mark, with the aid of Hjalmar Schacht, the President of the Reichsbank. An attempt was made to restore the economy. Once more the Social Democrats suffered. The communists determined to support them; their leader, Brandler, joined the socialist government of Saxony, which was then deposed by the Reichswehr, as was the socialist government of Thuringia. In Bavaria, the right-wing

The inflation in Germany advanced so fast that it was necessary to carry a box full of money in order to buy a loaf of bread. For a large part of the population this meant ruin. A soup canteen for the destitute. 1923

government was put under military control by Stresemann, whereupon the Nazi Party, founded by Adolf
Hitler in Munich in 1921, led a rising. The rising was
suppressed and Hitler was interned in a fortress. This
act of strength was followed by an improvement in
German affairs. Inflation was stopped; the Dawes Plan
stabilised the external value of the mark by meeting
debt repayments; the French left the Ruhr; and employment rose. The Social Democrats had left office. Ebert,
the President, died, and the election of 1925 showed
that the republican parties – the right, the centre, the
socialists, had over 22 1/2 million votes, while the Communist Party had only 2 million and the Nazis about
a quarter of a million. In 1925, therefore, the election
of 1924, which had given 3 3/4 million votes to the Communists and 2 million votes to the Nazis, was partially
annulled; stabilisation was working. After this came
the presidential election in which Hindenburg was put
forward as a right-wing candidate, narrowly defeating
the Centre Party's Wilhelm Marx. Hindenburg's
election was crucial. He detested the Republic; and he

was growing senile. In any crisis, therefore, he would back the Republic's enemies.

Nevertheless, by 1928, when another election was held, although the Nazis and the Communists gained votes, the Nationalists lost them, and the Social Democratic Party made a notable advance. It entered a coalition government with its leader, Müller, as Chancellor, and other socialists in key Ministries, like those of the Interior and of Finance. Yet, as in Britain, the socialist Finance Minister, Hilfarding, was a prisoner of the orthodoxies of public finance and of banking; he had no alternative to offer. None, indeed, existed. Hilfarding resigned in 1929 but his successor had no alternative either.

Once more the paradox of social democracy revealed itself. Committed to democracy, a victory in an election meant the victory of social democracy. Yet, in office, nothing happened. Nothing happened because they had no other policy to offer, than to govern well and humanely. But when the bottom falls out of the economy, that means running the labour exchange with a smile. The smile becomes a leer. The government falls.

Stresemann, the Centre Party leader, died in February 1930, as unemployment worsened. The Müller cabinet lost a vote of confidence in the Reichstag in March and was replaced by Bruning of the Centre Party. As unemployment rose, the fears of the German people of a repetition of 1923 became palpable. Support for the Nazis and the communists rose.

It was at this time that the Communists took the decision that the Nazis would prepare the way for communism, and rounded on the Social Democrats. In the face of these blows, and with unemployment amounting to many millions, the Social Democratic Party collapsed. In 1932 the Nazis polled over 13 million votes in the first election, and nearly 12 million in the second; by February 1933, when Hitler was already Chancellor, they polled over 17 million.

The Nazi Party had three great factors in its favour. It was patriotic – it repudiated the Treaty of Versailles, the traitors, the Jews, the pacifists – everybody who was against the German Reich of 1914. It intended to use the power of the state ruthlessly to eliminate unemployment and to maintain the value of the mark. In this it had the support of Hjalmar Schacht. And, thirdly, it had well-organised Storm Troops and Brownshirts, able to defeat the communists. The first meant that it had the support – or at least the willing abdication – of the army and the police. The second meant that it had the support of the working class and the petty bourgeoisie. The third terrorised the communists who, for once, were beaten at their own game.

The Nazis came to power in a coalition with Von Papen, but after the election of March 1933 they assumed total control. The trade unions were dissolved and replaced by a Labour Front. The Social Democratic Party was dissolevd in June 1933. Some of its leaders fled abroad, others were imprisoned. Many workers joined the Nazi Party while the Communist Party was declared illegal, and carried on its activities from Moscow.

The rise of the Nazis ended German social democracy as it had been known for over fifty years. They created a new kind of state – an industrial state, with full employment, based on terror abroad and at home. Its title – the National Socialist Party – was no accident. In many respects it was a socialist party. Unlike the communists, however, it did not expropriate the private owners. Unlike socialists, it was anti-international. The Social Democrats, even after the Nazi victory, behaved true to form. They voted for Hitler's foreign policy in the Reichstag; they resigned from the

The anatomy of defeat: posters from Germany in the 1930s, show how the Nazis came to power through the division of the opposition. By withdrawing support from the Social Democrats the Communists deliberately split the vote. **Left:** 'The Reichstag in flames; set on fire by the communists. The whole land would be the same if the communists and their fellows the social democrats were in power for even a couple of months . . . Crush Communism. Smash Social Democracy. Vote Hitler.' **Centre:** 'The People die under this regime (Nazi). Vote Social Democrat.' **Right:** 'Betrayed by the SPD (social democrats). Vote Communist'

Cartoon from *Simplicissimus* 1931. August Bebel, former leader of the social democrats looks down from the clouds to see socialism dismembering itself 'I don't recognise any socialists any more, I can only see divided factions'. By 1932 the split between the communists and social democrats had effectively destroyed the German left

Socialist International when it denounced the Nazis. German Nazism owed something to German social democracy. Nazism was cruel where the Social Democrats were ineffectual; it was efficient where they were incapable of rule; but both parties were nationalist. The big differences were in the attitude to the Weimar Republic, which was partly a Social Democratic creation, and to the Jews, from which group many Social Democrat leaders were drawn.

After 1933 German social democracy was dead. Its revival waited for fifteen years. But the example of its death was a signal to social democrats elsewhere of what fate held in store for them.

# Italy and Fascism

After unification in 1870 Italy remained a country that was still a collection of widely differing traditions, societies and economies. In the highly developed cities there were socialist movements, which were small; but to be nationalist was to be radical, and to be radical was to be anti-clerical. Thus, in the country of the Pope, political attitudes were determined by reaction to his stance. In such a context, the socialist movement was but one part of a nationalist, radical, anti-clerical movement.

In 1915 Italy entered the war on the allied side as a result of the secret London treaties, the purpose of which was to give the fringe of Italian territories under Austrian control to the United Kingdom of Italy. The war was at first disastrous, though the Italian army fought with great heroism, and victory was only achieved ultimately at very great cost of men and material. The dismemberment of Austria-Hungary did not fully satisfy Italian demands and expectations. By 1919, Italy was war weary, and felt that it had been tricked and led into a futile war. The war demands of the London Treaties were not met; yet the Italian socialists were 'renouncers' – that is, they wanted only Italian-speaking territories to be allocated to Italy. Thus, by 1919, Italian nationalism was in a highly confused and neurotic state, and the socialists had got themselves into a hopelessly false position. To these difficulties was added the classical dilemma. The Catholics had

**Above:** Postcard for a socialist congress in Italy. Marx with the red flag treads the Pope underfoot. A couple of priests flee into the distance where the sun of socialism is rising. In Italy the attitude to the church was always one of the chief factors defining a political view-point

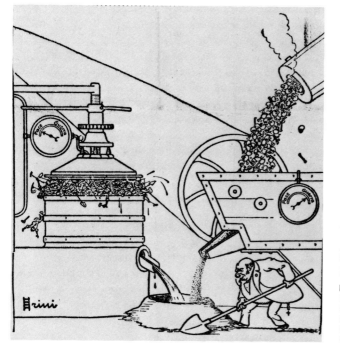

**Left:** 'From the blood of the workers and the bones of soldiers the capitalist prepares the cement to build his markets with'. Anti-war cartoon from the socialist newspaper *Avanti* in 1914. This was just after Mussolini had resigned from the editorship and shortly before his expulsion from the socialist party for supporting the war

not taken part in Italian politics because the secular Italian state was not recognised by the hierarchy; in 1918 the position was reversed and a Catholic Popular party was organised. Its strength lay in the countryside, and it make quick advances. The positive entry of the Catholic Church into politics was an important step, if only because it had the effect of driving the socialists into paroxisms of anti-clericalism.

The socialists were not only violently anti-clerical, they also adopted a revolutionary programme and posture, though they were totally unprepared for a revolution. Yet, closely allied to Moscow, they gained a large vote in the 1919 elections. The nationalists, however, inspired by people like d' Annunzio, were far more prepared for violence than the socialists. As the postwar economic problems intensified, industrial and social difficulties mounted. Mussolini, an ex-socialist, emerged as leader of the fascists, who were a mixture of nationalists, radicals and thugs. As the Socialist Party fell into increasing ideological difficulties, the fascist Blackshirts took over town after town, breaking up meetings, terrorising trade unions. Over all this trouble presided a series of ephemeral and hopelessly ineffective governments.

Fascism was violently patriotic and therefore violently opposed to the socialists, who were not only internationalists but were also manifestly dominated by Moscow. Fascism was violently anti-parliamentary, and parliamentary government was not working. Fascism was for strong state action to right social ills – and there were plenty of ills, including rural poverty and exploitation, unemployment, soaring prices and mass discontent. Mussolini thus became a hero of the masses, a rallying point for the army, a defender of the bourgeoisie (frightened of the large socialist vote in the industrial cities in 1919), and, oddly, a hero to the priests. The Popular Party, under the pressure of intolerable social unrest and seeking to outbid the socialists, had become too radical for the Pope. In 1922 he ordered all priests to leave politics, which literally took the heart out of the Popular Party.

Thus, in 1922, when Mussolini's Blackshirts 'marched' on Rome – it was actually an unopposed motorcade – they were welcomed by Pius XI as restoring order, welcomed by the bourgeoisie as preventing revolution, and welcomed by many of the poor as nationalist reformers.

Italian socialism was gradually made illegal and terrorised. In 1924 the socialist leader, Matteotti, was murdered. The trial of his murderers, who were fascists, was a farce; the guilty men were amnestied and opposition to the regime was suppressed. Tribunals were set up to try political offences; fascist labour unions replaced trade unions, and socialist leaders either emigrated or were imprisoned.

Mussolini's success was not only important in itself, because it put an end to Italian socialism for twenty years, but because it indicated an alternative path for Europe. Fascism was not originally an international movement, and it never became one in the sense that it was a centrally directed affair, like communism. It did, however, become an extremely important international fashion. It was authoritarian, and by stressing the importance of effective government it offered an alternative to the depressing political chaos into which many countries fell. It had a patriotic rhetoric which

Meeting in a factory occupied by workers in the summer of 1920. The industrial unrest which followed the election of 1919 took the form of increased trade-union and left-wing militancy which was only later crushed by the strong-arm tactics of the fascists

**Opposite:** Fascist supporters burning down the *Avanti* offices in 1922. Mussolini's march on Rome in this year was the beginning of the end for the socialists. Unable to organise a united opposition they were very easily suppressed by the blackshirts
**Below:** The body of Matteotti being carried away from the wood where it was found. In Italy, as elsewhere, the socialists failed to provide an effective opposition to fascism by being divided among themselves and then paid heavily for it Some socialist leaders left the country but in 1932 10,000 communists were arrested and in 1924 came Matteotti's murder, marking the final blow to the movement

was, for many people, infinitely more attractive than the rhetoric of internationalism. As the Third World revealed, from the 1940s on, nationalism was by far the most widespread political force of the twentieth century. Fascism laid emphasis upon national unity rather than upon class war and this, again, was attractive to those who disliked civil strife. It had a rhetoric – and possibly a genuine concern – for radical action to improve the lot of workers and peasants. It was, it claimed, socialism without the class war. It offered jobs and opportunities to the working class, especially in the armed forces and para-military formations, yet it did not attack the wealthy. Fascism started out as a variant of socialism, based chiefly on the working class; it became petit bourgeois; and it ended up as a front for powerful capitalists. Mussolini's emulators, especially Hitler, introduced anti-semitism and other detestable elements into their systems; but in the 1920s Mussolini's draining of the Pontine Marshes, his creation of autostrada, his efficiency, were not as reprehensible in the eyes of the outside world as they later seemed in a different and infinitely more vicious context.

# France

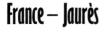

**France – Jaurès** The French social democrats were well-established and influential. *The Section Française de l'Internationale Ouvrière* (SFIO) was an attempt to unite the different French factions in the socialist movement. Disputes were frequent. But Jean Jaurès (1859–1914) was a leader who commanded great respect. Though he would have welcomed participation in bourgeois governments, he opposed those socialists who joined the French cabinet. The reason for this was important. The

Jean Jaurès speaking at a meeting in May 1913. As the editor of *l'Humanité* and the leader of the French socialist party Jaurès maintained unity with a policy of reform, antimilitarism, state monopolies and friendship towards the German people

French party regarded itself as internationalist and
anti-militarist; its very title indicated its position as a
local section of the Second International. Kautsky had
succeeded in getting the Second International to pass
a resolution declaring the aim of socialist parties to be
power, achieved by electoral procedures; but that participation in dribs and drabs in predominantly anti-socialist governments weakened rather than strengthened
the socialist cause. Since socialism represented a clear
break with liberalism and radicalism, rather than a
continuance with them, this doctrine was logical and
sound. But it ignored a central fact – that parliamentary politics required flexibility if they were to be successfully conducted, and that such flexibility might well
require coalitions, electoral arrangements and other

German cartoon
showing Jaurès killed
by a militaristic
French patriot: 'France
wanted freedom, but
killed the man who
opposed the war'.
Jaurès' policies earned
him the violent hostil-
ity of the French right.
He was assassinated
in 1914 and on the day
he was buried the SFIO
voted unanimously
for war credits

compromises, especially when the democratic regime
was itself in danger. After the fall of Napoleon III and
the repression of the Commune, the Third Republic
had virtually continuous instability. Despite the prosperity of France and its supreme achievements in civilisation, there were constant threats to the regime from
monarchists, from Boulanger, and from ex-Bonapartists.
The Dreyfus case epitomised the weakness of the
republic and its institutions, faced with the power of
the army; and for progressives (including socialists) the
vindication of the Republic against the anti-Dreyfus-
ards was of cardinal importance. Jaurès wished to save
the Republic, for if the sfio were to achieve a majority,
there had to be a republic for it to gain a majority in.
The Kautsky resolution, therefore, deprived him both
of flexibility and the means of helping the Republic.

Then came the First World War. It blew up suddenly, Jaurès was immediately assassinated by a right-
wing fanatic, and the socialists, viewing the German
social democrats (who mostly supported the war) as
traitors to internationalism, fell in behind the French
government. It was a case of national defence and
national defence was permitted to socialists. Two of
the leaders joined the government (Marcel Sembat and
Jules Guesde), and later Albert Thomas joined it as
Minister of Munitions.

As the war went on, however, and the terrible
slaughter of the French army occurred, opposition to it
began to mount. At first there was doubt about socialist participation in the government; also there was a
feeling that the war should be ended – a feeling
strongly encouraged by the Russian Revolution. The
French, as allies of the Russians, were deeply involved
in Russian affairs; and the apparent triumph of Russian socialism gave new hope to the French socialists,
for whom there was a prospect of a socialist conference to end the war and bring about a socialist (and
internationalist) peace. But at this point the socialists
split: the majority wanted to see Kerensky continue
the war; the minority, especially after the Bolshevik
Revolution, supported the Leninist demand for peace
and revolution. Strikes broke out, and once more
the French socialist movement was split. The socialists
refused to join Painlevé's government in September

Mayday cover of
*l'Assiette au beurre*
in 1906 demanding an
eight-hour day. It was
not to be won until
1919 and with the
Popular Front of 1936
France became one
of the first countries
to have a forty-hour
week and holidays
with pay

1917, and by October 1918 they were opposing war credits and were determined to support international socialist action to stop the war. But by then the war was ending.

Jean Longuet, Marx's grandson, was leader of the moderates. Like the German socialists, he supported the achievement of socialism by democratic and constitutional means, though at a quicker pace than Jaurès and other French socialists would have done. The reason for speed, of course, was the Russian Revolution and the imminence of socialism throughout the world. Above all, in contrast to the French socialists at the beginning of the war, the moderates blamed the war on capitalism and regarded the achievement of a just, socialist peace as their major political aim. The significance of Longuet's emergence as their leader with this posture was that the pro-Bolshevik revolutionary left was out-manœuvred and out-gunned; and the extreme left, in any case, consisted largely of syndicalists and quasi-anarchists. Thus when the war ended France was a completely non-revolutionary country.

The end of the war was marked by a trade union demand for a just peace, and for social and economic reforms, such as the eight-hour day. In 1919 there were mass demonstrations and Parliament passed the Eight Hours' Law, but in fact the trade unions were beaten. The French trade unions (organised in the *Confédération Générale de Travail* – CGT) were independent of politics, and therefore their defeat was not as politically significant as the defeats of the British trade unions. On the other hand, the Socialist Party was not rooted in the day-to-day struggles of the industrial workers: it was far more a debating society. Debates now raged about whether the SFIO should join the Third International – the Comintern. It was decided not to do so, but the debates helped to fracture the party and became even more fratricidal when it was badly defeated by Clemenceau in November 1919.

The main hall at the Congress of Tours, 1920. There are portraits of Jaurès on the wall inscribed 'Jaurès who died for you'. It was at this meeting that the SFIO voted to join the Third International and the split occurred between the social democrats and the group which then became the Communist Party

After a series of manoeuvres, the French sent a delegation to the Moscow Conference of the Third International. The delegation recommended that the SFIO should affiliate, and at the Tours Congress, in December 1920, an overwhelming majority voted to do so. The right wing thereupon left the party, which was transformed into the Communist Party. Thus the Communists became the major French working-class party, with all the party organisation, newspaper, and funds. The Congress had made French socialism communist just as the Emperor Constantine had made the Empire Christian.

The right wing (including the moderates) set up a new Socialist Party, handicapped by having no organisation but helped by the fact that most socialist Members of Parliament refused to become communists. The struggle from then onwards was between the Communist Party and the SFIO, with the Communists always on the attack. The government was strong; it defeated the trade unions in their great strike of 1920, and subsequently the French working-class movement degenerated into desperate groups of rivals. France was not a predominantly industrial country for the bulk of the population was engaged in agriculture. The working class was now weak and divided, leaving the socialists, who were the party of the intellectuals and school-teachers, with no effective electoral base.

The decline in French socialism caused the Communists to demand, in 1922, a united front of working-class parties, but the Socialists (who were becoming more and more a petit-bourgeois party) formed local electoral alliances with the Radicals. In France, to be progressive was to be anti-clerical and to support the principles of the Revolution; to be socialist was increasingly to be communist. The SFIO was thus progressive but not socialist. In the 1924 election the Communists were badly beaten, but electoral alliance with the Radicals gave the Socialists over a hundred seats in the Chamber. They gave support to Edouard Hérriot's Radical government which shifted French policy towards internationalism, evacuated the Ruhr, supported the Dawes Plan, and joined Ramsay MacDonald in the attempt to build up international institutions. Thus the Socialists, in supporting Hérriot, supported internationalism, and their popularity continued to increase, especially as the Communists sporadically expelled people who were not slavish followers of Moscow and who then rejoined the sfio. Some of these were Trotskyites, others became more orthodox social democrats. But whatever their views they strengthened the left in the sfio, and pressed (some of them, at least) for an electoral pact with the Communists. The main parliamentary strength of the sfio was prepared not only to support Hérriot but also to participate in a coalition with the radicals. However, they were unable to get party support to enter Poincaré's more solidly right-wing government, which stabilised the franc.

In the later 1920s France had not only a stable franc but, like America, genuine prosperity. In the circumstances it was difficult for any party arguing for major changes in society to gain a convincing vote. Thus in the 1928 election the Communists lost seats, while the Socialists, growing ever more respectable, just about held their own. Throughout the 1931 slump, which affected France less than any other major country, the parliamentary position was held, and in 1932 the Communists again lost seats, while the Socialists made small gains. There were frequent approaches to socialist deputies to join the Radical governments; and, though some of the deputies were more than willing, the party congress always refused permission.

Meanwhile the trade union movement, considerably attenuated, abandoned its revolutionary and syndicalist posture and concentrated on reforms. It was a small body, without significant power, and its members' allegiances were split between the Communists and the sfio.

All in all, the French Socialist Party, despite continual ideological disputes, contributed little to French life from 1914 to 1932. Its main contribution was to keep the main element of the petty bourgeois, small civil-servant vote in the republican arena and to support the Republic. The Republic was little threatened, however. France was peaceful, exhausted by the war, but victorious and reasonably progressive. It could look at defeated Germany's upheavals with contempt; and, with rapidly changing governments, it could look at

Mussolini's Italy with some interest but no great concern. Exhaustion and contentment, however, were not to keep the peace for long.

French prosperity continued well into 1932. The franc was stabilised by Poincaré in 1928 at a low level, and an export boom followed. But eventually the world depression became so severe that it spread to France, causing incomes to fall and a slight rise in unemployment. This was a situation that was to prove critical. Anti-clericalism in France had been important since Voltaire, but it is often forgotten how important clericalism, aristocracy and the right are too. France had an economic and social structure which had remained unaltered in substance, despite the changes in the legal structure that the Republic had brought about, and which left power firmly in the hands of the upper bourgeoisie. Thus, whenever the bourgeois Parliament seemed more farcical or corrupt than usual, powerful people turned their thoughts towards absolutism. France, in its days of glory, had been absolutist. The Third Republic, despite the cultural achievements of the civilisation over which it presided, had few claims to glory – for the war of 1914–18 had been won largely by the Allies and, in the last analysis, by the Americans. Had the French been alone it would have been another Sedan. In the circumstances, the Third Republic was, it seemed, a tawdry substitute for French glory. Ever since 1871 the upper bourgeoisie had attacked the Republic.

In 1922 Mussolini had brought a similar regime to an end in Italy. His style of fascism was attractive to advocates of 'sound government'. Italy seemed to be governed efficiently. The godless communists and socialists were suppressed. The Jews were discouraged from being too prominent in public life. The army and navy were strengthened and honoured. The French right, with its intellectual heroes, drawn to a sort of pessimistic eschatological view of the world, tended to support the *Action Française* of Charles Maurras and the *Croix de Feu* of De la Rocque, which were but pale reflections of militant reaction. But as Russian communism grew in power and horror, as Nazism revived

# France and Léon Blum

German militarism, and as fascist Italy 'put its house in order', more and more French people felt the need for a virile regime based on law, order, the Church and the traditional verities. On the left, the intelligentsia was communist and anti-clerical; on the right it was clerical and fascist; in the middle was the Republic, defended, it seemed, only by its corrupt politicians. The Stavisky scandal, which rumbled on from 1927 to 1934, implied that fraudulent financiers could be defended by politicians, including Prime Ministers, just as the army had been defended by politicians in the Dreyfus case, but for what to the right seemed infinitely less worthy motives.

The right grew more and more militant. Daladier came into office and, to gain SFIO support, dismissed the extremely right-wing *Préfet* of Paris, Jean Chiappe. In February 1934 the right-wing militants attempted to capture the Chamber of Deputies, during the debate on Daladier's justification of his actions. They almost succeeded. Daladier resigned. The immediate effect was a retort by the left in the form of strikes, organised jointly by communist and socialist trade unions. The

Léon Blum after winning the election of 1936. Though he set up the Popular Front, Blum was eventually defeated by the conservative interests in the Senate and was forced to resign

left, having seen the fall of the Weimar Republic, and seeing the rise of fascist Italy, was as ready to believe in an international right-wing conspiracy to overthrow republican institutions as the right was prepared to believe in an international left-wing conspiracy. The result of this confrontation was a great rallying of working people to the trade unions and the formation of the *Front Populaire* – a coalition – of socialists and communists, to fight fascism.

Throughout 1934 the Stavisky scandal continued to cause political disruption – soon after Daladier's resignation his successor Doumergue also resigned – while the economic situation deteriorated. When Britain went off the gold standard in 1931 France remained on it, and by doing so lost her competitive position in world markets. Exports fell, and workers and farmers suffered serious falls in income. The peasants thereupon became a strong addition to the right-wing forces. In this situation, the new Prime Minister – an

Slogans on the outside of the Communist Party Headquarters during the period of the Popular Front. This was based on an electoral alliance between the Socialists, the Radicals and the Communists who lent their support but did not join the government. The communist influence in the trade union movement (particularly the CGT) led to a series of increasingly radical demands

'ETAIT PREVU !

LE
COUP
DU SECATEUR

Cartoon about the devaluation of the franc from *Le Charivari* of 1936. The currency crisis in that year was said to have been partly engineered by financial interests who refused to do anything to solve it until the Popular Front government agreed to moderate its social programme and hand over leadership to the radicals

ex-socialist, Pierre Laval – increased the tension by intensifying the deflation: food prices fell and the peasants became more militant, initiating tax strikes. Laval, in order to placate the radicals, acted with increasing violence by suppressing the militant organisations like the *Croix de Feu*. Strangely enough, this firmness was successful, and the left strengthened its anti-fascist agitation.

Laval was in a difficult position. He was determined to maintain order and to preserve the franc. He was also acutely concious of German rearmament and of Italian demands for Nice and Savoy. He tried to keep the Nazis and fascists apart by agreeing to allow Mussolini to attack Abyssinia without French intervention, and in December 1935 he got the British Foreign Secretary, Sir Samuel Hoare, to agree to stop British sanctions, which had been invoked against Italy. The agreement was published and there was a strong British reaction against it. Hoare resigned and Laval's position was made far more difficult. In March 1936 the Germans reoccupied the Rhineland, making another war more likely, and in July 1936 General Franco rose in revolt against the Spanish Republic. France, with a discredited republican regime, a deflation, a militant right, and a communist-dominated left, was now surrounded by countries where military-minded dictators were on the march.

In mid-1936 the general election returned the sfio, under Léon Blum, as the largest party, and the Communist Party, as a result of the *Front Populaire*, also had seventy-two seats – a gain of sixty. Blum formed a government which the communists supported but did not join and which had radical ministers. It was the first major Popular Front government in the west, its support ranging from Marxists, both Trotskyite and Stalinist, to right-wing liberals. Immediately after the election a great wave of strikes broke out, for better industrial conditions. Blum forced the employers to accept their demands and enacted a forty-hour week and holidays with pay. His government opened, therefore, with the biggest single achievement of a socialist government in any major country. But, inevitably, price rises followed immediately and a devaluation of the franc had to be arranged. By June 1937 the reforms had to be followed by a 'pause'; a financial panic threatened and Blum resigned, to serve under a radical, Chautemps.

Meanwhile the Spanish Civil War raged. Blum followed the British in a policy of non-intervention. This not only left Spain to the mercies of the Italians, Germans and Russians, but alienated the left, especially the communists. The right were already furious with Blum, for being a socialist and a Jew, for his wage awards, and for not supporting Franco.

Chautemps had to devalue the franc a second time and, after the socialists had left office, he resigned, to be succeeded by Blum. The international situation deteriorated steadily. Hitler occupied Austria and threatened Czechoslovakia. Franco was winning in Spain. After a month, Blum resigned again and Daladier resumed office. It was his government that signed the Munich agreement, in September 1938. This was a momentous act. Not only did it show that Hitler could be refused nothing and that the British, French and Russians would not ally themselves against him, but it indicated that France could not act alone (as it had done in the Ruhr fifteen years earlier). Czechoslovakia was a close ally of France. By betraying the Czechoslovak cause the Daladier government destroyed their own international credibility.

Thus, by the end of 1938, the French were allied to Britain through the *Entente Cordiale*, they were nominally allied to the Soviet Union by the Franco-Soviet Pact of 1935, and they had enemies on all sides – Germany, Italy and Franco's Spain. Internally the Republic was despised by both the right and the left. The Socialists, after the great wage awards of 1936, had caused a series of major economic crises; and they had jointly presided over a collapse of French foreign policy.

War broke out in September 1939, almost by default, between Britain and France on the one hand and Germany on the other, nominally to defend Poland. The Russians and the Germans occupied Poland. From then on there was a lull until, in May 1940, the attack through Belgium led to the turning of the Maginot Line and the collapse of France. The government fell, an armistice was signed, and all but south-east and central France was occupied. The Socialist Party leaders were tried and imprisoned.

Thus the Third Republic collapsed, it seemed, from within. Its collapse was said to be due to bourgeois politics. The party that had been connected with it most was the Radical Party, but the SFIO had to accept a major part of the responsibility. The complete eclipse of French socialism seemed a fitting end to a sorry story. Yet within four years the Socialists were once more in office. The Resistance was the forcing bed of what seemed to be (though it was not) a new Socialist Party.

It can be seen that in the Third Republic the Socialists had no policy that was relevant, either internally or externally, to French problems. The reason for their lack of policy was twofold. First, the game of bourgeois politics in which they were involved was almost bound to be ineffectual, since the game bore little relevance to the real seats of decision-making which, in France, were always the permanent institutions of the Republic. These survived empires, republics, communes and Vichys, and were unaffected by socialist and radical politics. But, secondly, French socialism, like British and German socialism, had no coherent and powerful doctrine. Its policy was determined by a relationship to communist policy; to find a socialist policy, the SFIO looked at the communists then did the same, or not, as seemed fit. What a socialist doctrine might have been was to be revealed after the war.

The fall of France. Nazi troops march past the Arc de Triomphe as Paris is taken

# Constitutional rule and Socialist politics

In Britain the First World War had been immediately followed by an election in which Lloyd George had gained a big majority for his coalition. His majority was predominantly Conservative, drawn from the business and propertied classes. When they threw him over in 1922 the Labour Party increased its vote. In the election of 1923, it became the second largest party after the Conservatives, and with the promise of some Liberal support, Ramsay MacDonald became Prime Minister of the first Labour government.

The country which he was called upon to govern was already showing signs of the senescence which, within thirty-five years, was to bring its vast empire to an end. Two of the main troubles of the liberal era had ended with the achievement of self-government by Ireland and the granting of the suffrage to women, but the third great issue which had torn Britain apart before the First World War was even more important. This was the state of industry. Labour troubles were endemic.

They were endemic because the British economy was in a bad way, through it is important not to exaggerate the degree to which it was in a bad way. Throughout the 1920s and 1930s certain trades and industries grew. They were affected by the trade cycle but on average they prospered; electricity, telephones, light engineering, motor vehicles, housing, were some examples. For the greater part they grew in the mid-

## The General Strike

Striking miners
and their families
queue for soup in
the North of England
in January 1921

lands, around Birmingham, and in the south, around London. Thus the midlands and the south were relatively prosperous and the number of Labour Members of Parliament they elected small, those who were elected coming chiefly from the old slum or semi-slum districts like Stepney. In the north, in Wales, and in Scotland, on the other hand, the main industries suffered severe contractions in their markets – chiefly coal, heavy engineering, shipbuilding and textiles. The result was widespread unemployment, repeated attempts by employers to cut wages in order to avoid losses, and a general fall in the level of activity. In times of falling exports, and periods at the bottom of the trade cycle, the distress was severe.

Thus Labour drew its main support from these areas, where there was often deep suffering; and the split between the prosperous south (where the greater part of the middle class lived) and the north, was acute. The situation, in fact, resembled the position in the old United Kingdom, when the condition of Ireland was incomprehensible to the English and Scots. The

immediate postwar depression of 1920–1 revealed the
weakness of the British economy, which first led to
severe problems in the coalfields. The British export
markets had been partly lost as a result of the disrup-
tions of world trade caused by the war; their net surplus position in foreign trade had been jeopardised by
the liquidation of a number of investments and the
blows given to the export trade, while the instability
of the exchanges caused growing problems. The trade
unions in coal mining and other heavy industries, and
in the railways – that is, most of the leading manual
workers' unions – were involved in growing militancy, strikes and lock-outs. The Triple Alliance –

coal miners, railwaymen and transport workers –
lived in uneasy harmony, seeking to support each other
without jeopardising their own individual interests.
But the threat of a general strike of all trade unionists
was genuine enough; it had nearly been carried out
in 1914, again in 1919, and it remained a constant
menace.

The Labour Party in Parliament was predominantly
a trade union party, though its leader, J. R. Mac-
Donald was an intellectual. Its main role was to press
for social reforms, especially in the fields of social
insurance and working conditions, and to support the
trade union movement. Therefore, fear of the Labour
Party, on the part of the capitalist class, was partly a fear
of its trade union militants, for the weapon of the
general strike had been discussed for nearly a century
as the weapon for the inauguration of socialism. Yet
trade union militants in fact thought of the general
strike as a means of enforcing, by a general stoppage,
the wage demands (either for more money, or for the
restoration of a cut in wages) of one particular, threatened, group. Nothing could have been further from
their immediate thoughts than the overthrow of capitalism: their concern (legitimately and understandably)
was with pennies an hour. The other fear of socialism
stemmed from what was happening in Russia. The socialist movement had been all-embracing, so it was not
wholly unreasonable to assume, as middle-class people
did, that the comrades in Britain who sang the Red
Flag at Labour Party meetings had something in
common with the comrades in Moscow who sang the
Internationale at Communist Party meetings. In fact
the two groups had about as much in common as Jesuits
and Plymouth Brethren – both Christians in their
fashion. The Moscow communists had now organised
the Third International, which was busily penetrating
the Labour Party; and the Labour Party was fighting
back, though not, alas, penetrating the Third
International.

When Ramsay MacDonald became Prime Minister
his first aim was to find enough 'experienced' people
to be ministers and he therefore recruited a number of
office-hungry liberals. He also sought to give the impression that Labour was respectable enough to govern

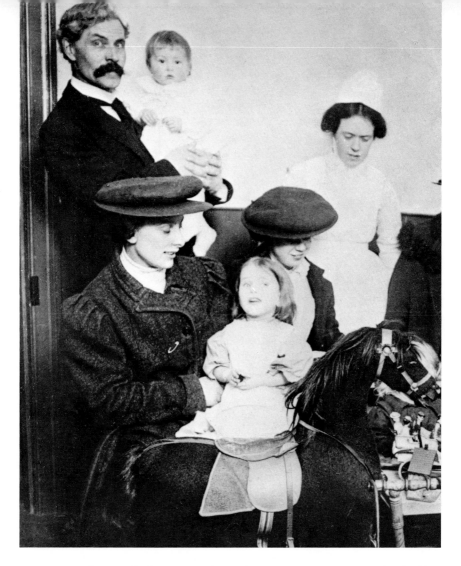

a great empire, and the governing class responded, much as they would have politely applauded a band of naked but loyal Africans rendering, by grunts and groans, a version of the National Anthem. For any legislative enactment, Labour depended on liberal support. For any radical measure the House of Lords had a two-year delaying power. It was therefore impossible for the government to be in any major sense radical. But it also suffered from the disadvantage that had it been in a position to do anything, it would not have had the least idea what to do.

Ramsay Macdonald opening a baby clinic. The problems facing the Labour government were huge, but its dependence on the Liberals and the two year delaying power of the House of Lords made it impossible for it to try anything radical in the way of solutions

The Labour Party had adopted a new constitution at the end of the war which declared it a socialist party. Proposals had been adopted for the nationalisation of the coal mines and the railways, and of a few other industries, but there was no possible executive mechanism for implementing them. At that time it was thought that an industry, once purchased by the government (for expropriation was ruled out) would be run like a government department –the Post Office, say – directly responsible to a minister who would in turn be responsible to Parliament. A growing body of younger opinion was frightened of the bureaucratisation involved in this notion and took a syndicalist line. Others still were Marxists and repudiated the notion that the state could run industry in a capitalist society. When socialism came, the state (that is the coercive powers of the state) would 'wither away' and industry would run itself.

Meanwhile, the Labour government enjoyed office. Virtually its only intellectual apart from Sidney Webb was the Prime Minister, an amiable man, greatly taken with office and its fruits. The Cabinet put on its top hats, went off to the social and business engagements that Cabinet Ministers had usually kept, and let the country drift along. And even if they had wanted to nationalise coal, or had been able to do so, what good it would have done the coal miners was not clear as the export market for coal was continually declining.

On the main issues of the day the Labour Party not only had no ideas but no viable ideas existed. Unemployment was a problem. There was no economist of serious standing in the world who believed that it could be cured except by cutting wages, or by cutting prices, or both. There was a tremendous amount of poverty. No serious economist in the world believed that public expenditure could rise significantly without cutting savings, depressing investment, and causing more misery. There was a crisis in international trade. Keynes argued that German reparations and the bad alignment of parities were the root causes of the trouble, but (even if he had been right) he was regarded as an eccentric. Nor, it must be pointed out, were the Marxist theorists in better case. All their predictions were

hopelessly wrong and Russia was staggering from
crisis to crisis, held together (as it had always been held
together) by tyranny. It was later to be shown that
unorthodox action was possible – Hitler in Germany,
Roosevelt in America, and Stalin in Russia – but the
first and the last of these used measures so barbarous
that they were wholly repugnant to all men of sense
and goodwill who knew what was going on. Indeed
trade union missions to Russia almost inevitably came
back disenchanted, except with particular instances
(health services, for example).

The Labour government fell in 1924, partly helped

The British Bulldog
pulling down the red
flag. Poster produced
by the Liberal Unionist
Council. In Britain
in 1924, as so often
elsewhere, the
opposition used
accusations of com-
munism to oppose a
social democratic
government

on its way by a series of stories that it was sympathetic to communism and that the communists were plotting to overthrow the consitution. There is no doubt that they were so plotting, but not only was their plotting ineffectual, it was mainly directed against the Labour Party. The Conservatives returned to office under Baldwin. The industrial situation continued to deteriorate. The mining industry fell into increasing difficulties as German coal, which had been stopped after the occupation of the Ruhr by the French, came on the market again and British exports fell further. The mine owners sought to cut mine workers' wages and a Royal Commission was appointed, which, to a great degree, supported such action in its report. The miners were locked out when they refused to accept the cuts; and the General Strike was called, on 3 May 1926. It was surprisingly widespread, though the trade union movement was almost totally unprepared for it. The government hastily organised emergency supplies and rallied support, greatly helped by its monopoly of the mass media (the strikers made a great mistake in closing down the newspapers), and on 12 May the General Strike ended, in wholesale defeat. There had been no Labour plans for the struggle, so it was scarcely surprising that the strike failed, but even if it had 'succeeded', what would 'success' have meant? The Labour Party was quite unwilling to overthrow the constitution and usurp power, yet the strike could only have been effective had the government resigned, which it

The edge of Hyde Park at 6 a.m. on the seventh day of the General Strike as armoured cars and troops prepare to escort a convoy of food lorries. There was little violence during the ten-day strike but the government used the opportunity to make a show of force to the striking workers

could only do following defeat in the House of Commons. And to have reversed the wage cuts would only have led to even faster falls in the sale of coal. Britain had revalued its currency by returning to the gold standard in 1925. Not a single Labour voice was raised against it – only Keynes's was – so that a successful strike while the country remained on the gold standard was a contradiction in terms: money wages would have risen, so would costs, sales would have fallen and so would employment.

Ramsay MacDonald and his government resumed office in 1929. This time they were the largest party in the House of Commons, though still not an absolute majority and still subject to the two-year suspensory power of the House of Lords. This time the Liberals were a less serious threat to them, electorally, though Lloyd George's campaign, inspired by some of the best minds in the country – notably Keynes's – was conducted on the basis of a programme that was to prove successful in Sweden and in the United States under Roosevelt. It is ironical that, had Lloyd George been elected instead of Ramsay MacDonald, and had that chronically dishonest but exceptionally able man carried out his programme, British liberalism might have preceded Swedish social democracy and the New Deal with a social democratic semi-Keynesian solution to the unemployment problem.

## The great betrayal-1931

MacDonald's government had three interrelated problems to deal with. The first was the international economic crisis. Almost simultaneously with the election, the New York stock exchange boom collapsed, and a cumulative panic seized the world money markets. By 1931, after the *Credit Anstalt* collapse in Vienna, the crisis was of a severity that surpassed anything that had happened before. The pound, as the world's leading trading currency, was continuously threatened, andthe Labour government was determined to maintain the gold standard. Their reasons for this were twofold: the respectable one was that they were told, and believed, that if Britain abandoned the gold standard, international trade would collapse, and the British export markets would disappear. The

## "WORKLESS"

disreputable reason was that they could not think of anything else to do, though Keynes and Ernest Bevin, the leader of the Transport and General Workers Union, had a plan for a managed economy that was to prove eminently satisfactory.

Against this background of growing international monetary crisis, the Labour government was struggling to maintain world peace. After the Versailles Treaty of 1919, the United States had retreated into isolationism. This settlement, left to Britain and France to police, had never worked well and came increasingly under strain. In 1923 and 1924 MacDonald tried hard to make the League of Nations effective. He and Arthur Henderson tried again in 1929–31. In those years the world came nearer to a universal peace settlement than at any time to come. Almost complete disarmament was achieved, except for Japan, but as troubles broke out, it was clear that no general settlement was capable of being held against determined aggressors: the Japanese in the Far East in the case of Manchuria; the Italians, when Mussolini came to power in 1922 with a doctrine of militant nationalism, and the additional threat of a revival of German militarism should Hitler and the National Socialists come into office. Ramsay MacDonald was justifiably vilified later for his helplessness in the face of the economic problem, but internationally his record was good. Had he been able to achieve an *entente*, acting through the League, it is just conceivable that the Second World War might have been averted.

The major crisis, however, which the government faced every day and neglected to tackle every day, was unemployment, which mounted steadily. As it grew, poverty and distress became more acute, especially in the Labour constituencies in Scotland, Wales and the north of England. Inevitably, payments out of public funds rose. They were insufficient to alleviate distress and their mode of disbursement – as a public charity – was humiliating and offensive to the unemployed, while the outflows were sufficient to alarm financial opinion about the state of the Treasury. Thus the government had two utterly irreconcilable pressures put upon it. The first was to alleviate its supporters' distress. The second was to keep public expenditure down in the hope of avoiding a loss of confidence in London as a financial centre. The tension was resolved by a complete capitulation to the need for confidence. Fundamentally this was due to the absence of any theory for coping with unemployment and to the absence of any boldness that was prepared to act without a theory. Margaret Bondfield, the Minister of Labour, was a weak and unimaginative politician. Philip Snowden, the trade unionist who was Chancellor of the Exchequer, was an ignorant and stupid man, determined to be as reactionary as possible. The left had no leaders. There was no pragmatic middle-of-the-road man to lead the Labour Party out of the horror. Sir Oswald Mosley, an attractive rising politician, resigned from the government but made the understandable error of starting a new party. It was not at that time fascist but its foundation meant that Mosley and his

supporters were no longer able to influence Labour policy. The political pressures on the government were all reactionary. The Conservative Party was deeply worried about the national finances. The Liberal Party made the government pass an Anomalies Act which reduced the number of unemployed able to claim benefit, pushing the unfortunate people straight into the arms of the Poor Law.

Meanwhile, throughout 1931, attempts were made to secure foreign loans, while the government did literally nothing about the economy and virtually nothing about social reform. It is difficult to see what they could have done, given the limitations of the ideas prevalent at the time. The only intellectual alternative to laissez-faire was Marxism and (it must be emphasised) what was happening in Russia at that time gave no indication that Marxist-Leninism offered any alternative save revolutionary terror. It must be recalled too, that, though bad, conditions were not as bad as all that in large parts of the country. The falling price level meant that people in safe jobs (teachers, civil servants) or in prospering industries, were increasing their real incomes steadily. Only in the crisis years 1931–2 did many of their incomes fall, both in money and real terms. And people with capital, however little, had a great deal to lose if capital values collapsed. Prudence dictated, therefore, the avoidance of panic or of unorthodox measures that inclined people towards panic. Britain was still a free-trade country. Any drastic attempt to raise employment would have entailed not only going off the gold standard but a significant shift to protection and, probably, to controls on capital movement. By 1936 Britain had done the first two, and

Germany had done all three; but five years is not an exceptionally long time when ideas and attitudes are involved.

Labour's policies and views from 1929 to 1931 profoundly affected opinion about social democracy. In the first place, a number of people, like Mosley, came to the conclusion that a quasi-military organisation of society, such as Mussolini had achieved in Italy, was necessary to bring Britain back to greatness. In Germany, where the depression was far worse and militarism more popular, many social democratic voters went over to Hitler. In Britain a few intellectuals went over to communism but most people did not. It is interesting to speculate why. Life in Britain was not too bad. Life in Russia, especially with the famine in the Ukraine, was terrible; and the ghastly irony of Stalin's 'Comrades, life is better, life is brighter' speech, while millions starved, thousands were in prison, and thousands were shot, was not lost on the British working people. But, above all, when the Conservatives came back into office, in September 1931 (under the guise of a National government), economic recovery began, first by abandoning the gold standard and adopting protection, and secondly by a housing boom, largely resulting from low interest rates, which in turn were due to Neville Chamberlain's sensible policy at the Treasury. From 1931 until the middle of the Second World War, Labour not only had no real alternative programme to offer to pragmatic conservatism, but it was exceedingly doubtful whether it could govern at all, since its record from 1929 to 1931 had been so miserable. When Labour's fortunes were restored it

A skirmish between police and unemployed in High Holborn, London during a demonstration in the summer of 1931

was largely because of foreign and social policy, and the economic policy advocated was contrasted not with Chamberlain's success at the Treasury but with Lloyd George's disasters in 1921 and Snowden's in 1931. Thus were the Conservatives blamed for a Liberal and a Labour failure.

The mode of Labour's collapse in 1931 was dramatic and the very substance of myth. As the summer wore on, unemployment mounted and foreign confidence fell. Foreign loans helped to support the pound. Then a committee under Sir George May reported that substantial cuts were necessary in social expenditure,

National Government election poster of 1931. Labour's total failure to cope with the slump dealt a great blow to socialism in Britain

including unemployment relief, if the pound were to be saved. The government was in agony; ministers tried to avoid the implications of the cuts and it was rumoured that the Cabinet was split. This promptly caused foreign confidence in the pound to wane still further, for it was feared that a Labour government might ignore the May Committee's recommendations. It is now known that this rumour was untrue. The Cabinet was in fact united on the principle of cutting expenditure; the argument was about where the cuts were to fall. As the crisis grew more desperate Mac-Donald and Snowden formed the opinion that the only hope was to form a coalition to save the pound; after the pound was saved, it appears that he hoped to resume normal party arrangements and, presumably, to re-appear as a Labour leader. Yet he took no serious steps to tell his colleagues, or the Labour Party, that this was his intention. He went to the King, came back and dismissed his colleagues, and formed a new government. The Labour Party was hopelessly split: a rump supported MacDonald but the great majority voted to expel him and the rump from the Labour Party. The new government went off the gold standard. It won a vast electoral victory; the Labour Party was virtually wiped out, having only 46 Members of Parliament, including only one ex-Cabinet Minister, George Lansbury, an insignificant figure of some moral stature, who became the leader. But Labour, leaderless and defeated, had a valuable alibi. MacDonald had always been a traitor, it was said, and he had long since planned to do a deal. Betrayed not defeated, Labour could console itself. The fact that it had no policies at all was conveniently forgotten.

## Labour 1931-38

The defeat of 1931, reducing the Labour Party to 46 Members of Parliament, and giving the Conservatives an overwhelming victory, could have led to the complete disappearance of the Labour Party. A scenario may be imagined in which the steady improvement in economic conditions that followed the bottom of the slump in 1932 was followed by a widespread adoption of Keynes's ideas, advanced in *The General Theory of Interest, Employment and Money,* in the winter of 1935-6, and representing an intellectual breakthrough of the greatest importance on the question of how to manage a capitalist economy in order to achieve full employment. Had the ideas been adopted, say by 1940, as they were increasingly (in Sweden and in America particularly), then the radical commitment to a social democratic party might have disappeared. A party system would have survived but it would (perhaps) have been far more like the American or German party system in the 1960s, or the British party system before 1914. It may well be the case, indeed, that British politics in the 1960s provided a justification for this view: that in a post-Keynesian economy, a social democratic party had no distinct ideological basis. That it was not so in the 1930s was due almost entirely to the international situation and to the slowness of the recovery from the depression. A great deal must be attributed, too, to the power of party loyalty. Studies seem to have shown that the pattern of voting loyalty, once established, is hard to break. Labour had established itself, before 1931, as the party for which over half of the manual working class habitually voted. In 1935 this pattern re-established itself, as indeed it probably would have done in 1931 had a few months – or even weeks – elapsed between the 'betrayal' by MacDonald and the election, so that the Labour Party could have adopted candidates and prepared to fight the election.

The period up to 1935 was largely preoccupied by the problems of the unemployed and the impoverished. Despite the drift towards communism of a number of intellectuals, from Kim Philby, the master-spy, to John Strachey, and the Webbs, the bulk of the intelligent working class rejected the Soviet Union as a system of terror sustained by lies. The preoccupation of the Labour Party was with social welfare and, in this connection, its victory in the London elections in 1933 was important. Herbert Morrison became the leader of the London County Council, the biggest local authority in the country, and promptly began to press through small but important reforms. Thus, increasingly, Labour turned to the practicalities of government. Herbert Morrison, who had been Minister of Transport from 1929 to 1931, was also the originator of another pioneering piece of work. A bill of his to establish a public board to own London Transport – the London Passenger Transport Board – was enacted by the National Government, and it established the procedure by which industries and services could be taken into public ownership in the Labour government of 1945–51. A board was established which ran the industry, under an Act of Parliament, generally subject to the Minister's directions but independent in its day-to-day operations, which were carried out on normal commercial principles. Thus Herbert Morrison, by putting London ahead in social welfare, hospitals and education, and by establishing a model of a statutory board, set the pattern for social development.

When to this was added the development of the techniques for maintaining full employment, Labour by 1938 had a domestic strategy for economic and social development which was wholly in advance of the strategy with which it had faced the experience of the 1931 depression. There was also the experience of Sweden and of Roosevelt's New Deal to show that radical governments could defeat the bankers and could use the power of the government to undertake significant programmes of economic development and social reconstruction. The atmosphere had changed significantly; a new generation had arrived which no longer believed in laissez-faire, which no longer saw Bolsheviks under the bed when socialism was discussed, but (paradoxically) thought of Roosevelt and the Swedes.

But the biggest change of all was the darkening international situation in which there were a number of separate issues that brought the Labour Party support. They were virtually incompatible but each had such moral overtones that the diversity was swamped by a bellowing of righteousness, which had the immense advantage of putting the Conservative government in the wrong whatever it did, whether it rearmed or disarmed, whether it appeased Hitler or was bellicose to him, whether it intervened in Spain or whether it did not. The first of these causes was the League of Nations and disarmament. MacDonald had an excellent record internationally, in his support for the League and in his campaign for international disarmament. Henderson, the Foreign Secretary in the 1929 government, remained as chairman of the international conference on peace in Geneva, which finally adjourned, with Henderson dying and nothing achieved. But the belief remained that if the League were strengthened peace could be maintained, and the League of Nations Union and the Peace Pledge Union jointly showed how enormous was the support for an active policy to build up the League of Nations. The celebrated 'King and Country' debate at Oxford, when the Oxford Union voted by a majority that it would not fight for King and Country was not primarily a pacifist motion; it was in fact a vote that they would only fight for an

Social democrats being rounded up in Vienna during the bloody events of February 1934, in which a socialist revolt, triggered off by anti-socialist measures, was savagely repressed by government troops. Shortly afterwards the Austrian Socialist Party was banned

international cause. But support for the League was also connected with pacifism. Lansbury, the leader of the Labour Party, was a pacifist, as had been Ramsey MacDonald, and the pacifist feeling was widespread as a revulsion after the horrors of the First World War and from a sense that it had been utterly unnecessary – merely due to dim politicians and corrupt generals – and had settled no substantive issue. On the other hand, those who wished to use the League to deter aggression had necessarily to argue for rearmament.

After 1934 this became a live issue. The social democrats were the first victims of the German Nazis, also of the terror in Vienna waged by Nazi sympathisers against the social democratic authorities. As refugees fled to Britain, Labour Party leaders like Hugh Dalton realised that German militarism would once more have to be fought, and pressed for rearmament. Then after the 1935 election Ernest Bevin took the issue to the Labour Party Conference and overthrew Lansbury. Thenceforward Labour was in principle committed to armaments, though in practice every step towards rearmament was opposed. The arguments for opposing it were not entirely specious: it was feared that the National government would use the arms not against the Nazis but against the communists. It was argued, therefore, that before rearmament could proceed, foreign policy would have to be changed.

The Spanish Civil War brought this issue to a head. The British government adopted a policy of non-intervention. As the Spanish army was in revolt, and it was aided by Italy and Germany, the Republican government was almost bound to lose, especially as Russian support was feeble and the Republicans were themselves split up into four major groups, with the Stalinists more anxious to attack their allies than the enemy. Inexorably the Falangists – the Spanish fascists – swept across Spain, and the heroic resistance of the Spanish people served only to prolong the agony. The war grew more barbarous, and Guernica, where for the first time aerial bombardment was used as a weapon of terror against a civilian population, showed what a future war would be like. Social democrats rallied to support the Republic and some brave spirits went off to fight in the Major Attlee Battalion of the International

Brigade. Labour was aware of a fascist axis of Germany and Italy, determined on aggression and turning on the social democrats with terror. As the anti-semitic persecution intensified in Germany, the Jewish refugees added to Labour's feelings, since the Jewish community was by tradition a Labour group.

The Comintern changed its policy in 1936 and supported the notion of popular fronts against fascism. Its earlier policy had been one of welcoming the destruction of bourgeois reformers. Consequently, no love was lost between the two parties. On the change of policy, the British communists sought to set up a popular front which would press ahead with a military alliance between Russia, France and Britain. The Labour Party indignantly rejected it, supposing (correctly) that this was but one more tactic of infiltration. With the Spanish Civil War lost, with rearmament proceeding apace, and with the humiliation of Munich when the British Prime Minister signed away Czechoslovakia's frontiers to Hitler, Labour became even more aware of its place as a British radical party, whose duty it would be to rally the country against totalitarianism.

The signatories of the Munich agreement. From left to right: Chamberlain, Daladier, Hitler and Mussolini

When, in 1939, the Nazi-Soviet Pact was signed, the Labour leaders felt justified in their forebodings about the communists. Despite the fact that some of the best Labour people had been expelled from the Labour Party because of the popular front issue, the party was united in its view of Hitler and Mussolini.

Thus, from 1931 to 1939, Labour had become a national party once more. It had a domestic policy and in a muddled way, it had a patriotic foreign policy, which was to be its best guarantee of future success. Hitler and the communists hated the social democrats. They hated Hitler and Stalin, in turn, which was understandable and right.

In the United States the socialist movement was always weak. Trade union leaders came from European traditions, and tried to form a socialist movement. Populist movements sprang up. There were Utopian settlements. But there was no general socialist movement. The immigrant working class was organised politically in its local wards; many of the ward bosses

## The New Deal

were integral parts of the Democratic Party, though the Republican Party, with its deep roots in the northern struggle for the Union also attracted many working-class supporters. America was democratic, and it seemed an open society, with great opportunities. To the European left, America was for long a promised land; and the European left, the American populists, and American legislators were equally disturbed by the growth of the great monopoly capitalists. Thus, in the European socialist mind America had a dual role: it was the land of opportunity and democracy; it was also the land of monopoly capitalism. Marxists attempted to account for this paradox by maintaining that the closure of the frontier had turned extensive exploitation into intensive exploitation and that the poor immigrants and the poor Negroes represented the exploited proletariat. America would increasingly become characteristic of monopoly capitalism.

Yet, while Europe was in turmoil during the early

President Franklin Delano Roosevelt at a baseball game. With his great personal courage and his New Deal policies he came to symbolise the possibility of recovery from the trials of the thirties

1920s, America was not. Prosperity grew steadily, and then almost frenziedly as the age of the automobile swept in. There were considerable improvements in the American standard of living. Republican presidents were elected on a 'business as usual' ticket and all (superficially) went well until the first year of the Hoover administration, when in 1929 the stock market collapsed. Immediately investment fell off and unemployment mounted. After a plateau in 1930, a rapid decline began which became a rout. By 1932 many millions were unemployed, a great many investors had lost everything, and undernourishment and acute poverty were widespread. Hoover and his administration sought to face the situation by restoring business confidence. Needless to say, they failed.

Roosevelt won the Democratic nomination. He symbolised, as a cripple paralysed by poliomyelitis who had overcome his handicap, the overcoming of tribulation. This is not as fanciful as it might seem, since his campaign was rhetorical rather than practical. He campaigned, for example, for a balanced budget and a sound currency, which would have been disastrous; yet his appeal was that of somebody who would do something.

When he was inaugurated in 1933 the American economy was almost at a halt. In Europe, too, things were at their worst. Hitler was returned to power in just such circumstances. What Roosevelt did in his first hundred days (the comparison with the return from Elba to Waterloo might have seemed unfortunate), and in his New Deal, was to undertake a series of wildly contradictory actions, many of which worked, and for which a *post hoc* theoretical explanation had to be given. Roosevelt was not a Keynesian – regarding Keynes with hostility as an impractical theorist – but he accidentally undertook Keynesian policies, by massively increasing public expenditure, both on social welfare and on public investment, and by unbalancing the budget. This, together with his other measures to restore the confidence of the American people in themselves, 'worked' in the sense that unemployment fell substantially and that profits and prices recovered. How much of this was due to the normal recovery of the trade cycle, how much to Roosevelt, how much to

Cartoon from the Chicago *Tribune*. The New Deal policy, by allowing a certain amount of state intervention in America's affairs, led to Roosevelt being accused of 'socialism' and a betrayal capable of undermining the constitution

international action (which was gradually reviving world trade on the basis of managed currencies and high tariffs) it is difficult to say.

What is important, however, is that Roosevelt represented the third possibility of recovery from the collapse of capitalism – Hitler and Stalin being the others. He had the immense merit of being the leader of a great constitutional democracy and of using the power of the democratic state to restore the economy, to introduce welfare services and to recreate confidence. In essence what he did was not dissimilar to what governments were doing elsewhere – Baldwin and Chamberlain in Britain, for example – but it was the manner in which it was done that mattered.

In the American context Roosevelt was left wing. Seen across the Atlantic it was easy to portray the Democratic Party as a social democratic party (which, of course, it was very far from being). Roosevelt was an orthodox liberal, somewhat to the right of Lloyd George, but he was represented as being almost socialist.

His attacks on business orthodoxy, seen out of context, seemed socialist. The landmark of his administration that was seized upon was the Tennessee Valley Authority – the TVA – which used public investment to restore a derelict area. It became a place of left-wing pilgrimage. In fact the dams, the electricity generators, the housing, the soil reclamation, though important in themselves were a relatively minor part of Roosevelt's New Deal. But in the 1930s, when business orthodoxy was so tired and so dim, rhetoric and symbol was everything.

Similarly with Roosevelt's international policy. Until well on into 1940, America remained profoundly isolationist. Roosevelt, as a liberal patrician, was deeply shocked by Hitler and the other fascists, and he saw increasingly that in a world war America would inevitably be involved on the anti-Axis side. But he had to move circumspectly and extraordinarily cautiously. His rhetoric was important: he was given to peace moves, to appeals to Hitler, to proposals for conferences. What would have stopped Hitler would have been treaties and troops, but they had to wait until Hitler was foolish enough to declare war on America after the Japanese attack on Pearl Harbour in December 1941. Roosevelt earned, however, the entirely unjustified reputation of an active and ferocious anti-fascist, whereas poor Chamberlain (who, after all, did declare war on Hitler twenty-seven months before Hitler declared war on Roosevelt) was denigrated. The reason for this was that Roosevelt was the democratic hero and was assumed to have taken actions and positions that Europeans would have wished him to take. In this respect, the Republican attacks on Roosevelt for being both a socialist and an internationalist helped to invent a Roosevelt who never existed.

The significance of Roosevelt and the New Deal for the social democratic left was twofold. In America, apart from the communist conspirators there were hardly any socialists. To be on the left was to be a New Dealer. Elsewhere, to be a socialist meant increasingly to be a New Dealer, that is to adopt the policies, often imaginary, that were supposed to be part of the New Deal. Deficit budgeting, comprehensive redevelopment of depressed areas, social welfare

'Yes, You remembered me'. A New Deal eulogy. Roosevelt shaking hands with the forgotten man. This kind of populist touch was sometimes mistaken for socialism

measures, control of the banks and the stock market –
all these seemed to be part of a socialist rather than a
liberal programme. Partly this way due to the style of
the New Deal which was essentially populist. Its verbal assaults on bankers were in the populist tradition;
its zeal for the ordinary man was extraordinarily per-
suasive. Thus by 1936 or so a social democratic government that came to office in Western Europe had a
policy, and a model – Roosevelt's New Deal.

# Sweden and Denmark

Scandinavia was an island of security in the 1930s.
With a long tradition of rural prosperity and constitutional rule, it consolidated a prosperous democratic
system in the early decades of the twentieth century.
Sweden, as a major industrial country, provided a model which reconciled social democracy with industrial
progress. It suffered less from the slump than other
countries, partly because its timber, wood pulp, and

iron exports kept up both in volume and price, and partly because its economists devised, very early, counter-depressive measures. The great Swedish economists came (by another route) to the same conclusion as Keynes, that public expenditure could create employment. Sweden inherited a system of social security, on the Prussian model, which kept public expenditure up and like other Napoleonic countries it had a more than century-old tradition of major public works expenditure. When, in 1920, the Social Democrats became the largest party and formed a government, they had around them all the components of a post-Keynesian welfare state – pensions, a health scheme, an excellent education system, extensive public works – and it remained only for them to endorse the principle of unbalanced budgets. So successful were the Social Democrats in this policy that they were re-elected with an increased vote in 1921 and thereafter remained continuously in office.

The second Swedish Social Democratic government, formed in October 1921. Seated (from left to right) are F. W. Thorssen, the Minister of Finance, H. Branting, Prime Minister and Foreign Minister, and Herman Lundquist, Minister for the Social Services

Similarly, in Denmark a Social Democratic government was in office (in a coalition) from 1920, following essentially the same policy, though as Denmark had a very small industrial sector the agricultural policies of the government were central to its success. Denmark's agriculture rested upon a strong co-operative basis. By the use of co-operatives, and with state aid, Danish agriculture was kept technically ahead of the rest of

Scandinavia had a long and respectable tradition of workers' movements. Danish Mayday demonstration in 1914, demanding an eight hour working day

Europe; and it was able to supply the growing British market for eggs, bacon and dairy products at decreasing prices.

Denmark, therefore, represented a rural society based on co-operative principles, utterly at variance with the collapse of industrial societies based on *laissez-faire*. The pure air of Scandinavia, the Oslo breakfasts of milk, fruit and eggs that produced tall, tanned,

Photograph of Copen-
hagen school children
from *Picture Post*
magazine, captioned:
'among the best fed
children in Europe
today'. The achieve-
ments of the
Scandinavian system
were used throughout
the world to proclaim
the potential of post-
war social democracy
and the welfare state

lithe, strong-toothed children, using well-designed wooden furniture and living in garden suburbs, all contrasted with the rickety, toothless populations that inhabited the hideous industrial slums of capitalist Europe. Scandinavia (like New Zealand) offered healthy living, with low infantile mortality rates and tremendous social and some aesthetic achievements.

The pull of the Scandinavian ideal cannot be overestimated. Scandinavian health, education, social welfare, housing, and architecture – no mean indices of a standard of living – were streets ahead of the rest of Europe. That this was achieved by Socialist governments, following non-orthodox fiscal and monetary policies, was no less important for other social democratic movements than were the achievements of the New Deal.

# India

The Third World War of developing nations, which was to play so large a part in the politics of the mid-twentieth century, was very much offstage in the 1920s and 1930s. The European colonial rivalries of the later Victorian years had gone, save for Hitler's rhetorical demands for the return of the German colonies sequestered at Versailles, and Mussolini's conquest of Abyssinia. Nationalism was chiefly centred in the successor states to the Austro-Hungarian Empire. In Africa and Asia it was barely stirring. The Chinese war lords were struggling for the control of China, Indian nationalists made periodic disturbances that got into the newspapers, but of general and widespread symptoms of colonial revolt there was no sign. According to Lenin, the colonial empires represented the source of profit to imperialist monopolists who had exhausted their profitable opportunities at home, and this was the accepted socialist reason for the existence of the empires. It was to remain the accepted interpretation, especially by the nationalists; indeed it was believed by the Labour British Foreign Secretary, Ernest Bevin, who was determined to keep bases in the oil-bearing Arab states in order to defend the standard of living of British workers. There is in fact little evidence that beyond the normal profits of trade there was any significant degree of exploitation of colonial empires by colonial powers. Political regimes and defence forces, as in India, were paid for by taxes on the indigenous populations; the French, especially, and to a lesser degree the British, particularly after the tariff reforms of 1931, gave advantages to their own businesses; the Belgian state and Belgian companies appear to have transferred funds substantially from the Congo to Belgium; but there was no evidence of general exploitation, in the sense in which treasure was looted from Latin America by the Spanish in the sixteenth and seventeenth centuries. Wages were low in Africa and Asia, but so was productivity. Minerals were extracted on a vast scale from South Africa and other territories but this was not in itself evidence of exploitation. The terms of trade of primary products fell as against manufactured products, but that was because of the depression. The export earnings of Africa and Asia were depressed. The falling prices of food and raw materials greatly helped those in the metropolitan countries who were in employment. On the other hand, the profits of businesses which dealt in primary products and those of the planters, the miners, and the agriculturists were diminished and in many cases eliminated by the falling prices.

Out of all this, it is difficult to demonstrate any significant degree of truth in the Marxist contention about imperialism. It was connected with trade and, like all trade between unequal partners, it could result in exploitation. But imperialism seems to have been chiefly what it appeared to have been, one nation imposing its will on another, for reasons that varied but which were in essence political (in the non-Marxist sense).

Gandhi spinning at a nationalist demonstration in Calcutta in 1925: the spinning wheel was a symbol of the return to simplicity and self-discipline which he advocated

What imperialism did was to establish firm and, to a degree, modern government, and to engender, by a reflex process, a series of nationalist movements whose purpose became one of taking over the government rather than one of sending the imperialists packing and reverting to pre-imperialist conditions. This was especially important in India, where large parts of the country were governed by British-protected princes, and in British Africa, where tribal chieftains and emirs also ruled directly, under British suzerainty. Modernisation meant opposition to these rulers.

Indian nationalism had four aspects. One, which was unimportant, was agitation for greater independence by the princes, especially when they had been stopped from doing something outrageous to their own subjects. The second was opposition to British rule by modernising politicians, often British-educated, who wished to take over the British functions. Third, there were modernising politicians who were also socialists. These people, like Nehru, wished to use the British-created state to eliminate social evils (like untouchability) and to promote economic development. It was they who were represented as a major threat both to the British and to the Indian princes. Last, there were the religious leaders, like Gandhi, who wished to use the nationalist movement to lead India to a Tolstoyan, Utopian society which wholly rejected modern industrialism and which would be based on the simple life of ascetism, agriculture and handcraft industries. Though the Gandhians and the socialists made common cause, their aims were in fact in great conflict.

It was Gandhi who, by the doctrine of non-violent resistance, fasts to death, and the organising of systematic unrest, became the leader of Indian nationalism. Despite the opposition of influential conservatives, both Labour and Conservative governments gave India considerable degrees of autonomy by 1935; but Gandhi and his supporters continued to work for complete independence.

By this agitation, Gandhi made two contributions to socialism: firstly, he brought the problems of colonialism and imperialism to the forefront of British opinion (there was no comparable shift in France), and secondly he offered a Tolstoyan brand of socialism to the world, which (by a process of assimilation) seemed to have more in common with social democracy than with communism. By 1936 the independence of India was in sight. The links between Indian and British socialists were close. It was possible that the developing world would choose socialism and not communism.

Thus nationalism, Gandhi's doctrines, and socialism came together – just as forty years before, vegetarianism, mysticism, Irish nationalism and socialism had been linked. The British left, especially, was anti-colonialist, because of its opposition to tyranny and its dislike of the governing class that found so much to do in the Empire. The old concept of radical imperialism had died, though it was very strong in France. The French Revolution had always been for export, especially since Napoleon's conquest of Europe; the French left remained convinced that France had a civilising mission in North Africa, Central Africa, the Levant and Indo-China, and that a rise in the standard of living could be achieved by French state action. These radical differences of approach were to be revealed after 1945.

# The War

In many ways it was not the slump, nor the Second World War, that was the big element in the development of the social democratic posture in the late 1930s and the 1940s, but the Spanish Civil War. That this was so was not because of Spain itself but because of the forces that intervened there. Spain became a symbol and a myth. The story of the Civil War became a saga of the socialist movement – a saga that had something, but not much, to do with what actually happened in Spain.

## Spain and the Civil War

In the 1930s Spain was a relatively backward and stagnant nation, socially and politically. Barcelona was the only really developed industrial city, and it was the home of a local nationalist (or federalist) movement, which had anarchist doctrines based on Proudhon, Sorel and Bakunin. In the 1920s the anarchists were attempting to crush industrial development. The constitutional monarchy was increasingly ineffective. Primo de Rivera, the military dictator, took over as a mayor of the palace and in the late 1920s, as world trade grew, Spain seemed increasingly prosperous and peaceful. The Spanish socialists had fought the usual struggle about communism and had not joined the Comintern. They supported Primo de Rivera and helped him to develop trade unions. Thus, in some respects, Spanish socialists were almost prototype fascists – national socialists, supporting a strong government, using the government to strengthen the trade unions, and supporting a national dictator. However, within a few years they were to join the other forces of the left in the Civil War against Franco and the Falange.

In 1930 the king dismissed Primo de Rivero. In 1931 the monarchy itself fell and a republic was established which removed some of the Church's privileges, expropriating (with compensation) some big estates and forbidding teaching by religious orders. In Spain neither the Church nor the army supported the constitutional

monarchy and they detested the Republic. As the economy deteriorated with the slump, Spain increasingly
fell apart. There were two brands of monarchists –
Carlists, intensely reactionary, Alfonsists, slightly less
so – and there were also fascists, drawing on the example of Mussolini (successfully governing a Latin
country), the army (colonels and generals), the Catholic centre, the communists, the anarchists, the regional
nationalists, the traditional political parties, and the
social democrats. In 1933 Primo de Rivera's son José
entered politics, founding the Falange Español, which
was fascist – believing in 'national unity', in violence,
and in repression of atheistic communism (which included almost everybody who was not a militaristic,
totalitarian, credulous Roman Catholic).

In 1933 a right-wing government came into power
and began to undo the reforms; revolts broke out and
the situation deteriorated rapidly. The Falange was
small and powerless, until in 1936 the Popular Front
of the left won the election against the Catholic-monar-
chist National Front. The generals and the Carlists
plotted to overthrow the Republic. In this they were
joined by the Falange. José Primo de Rivera was imprisoned and when the rising occured in July 1936
he was shot. The Falange thus became the political
expression of the revolting generals, though Franco
became Head of State without discussion with the
Falange.

The overthrow of the Spanish Republic was, therefore, mainly military. Yet to the outside world it
seemed a part of international fascism, partly because
Mussolini and then Hitler supported Franco, and because the communists, rallying to the support of the
Republic, denounced the generals as fascists.

Even the phrase 'rallying to the support of the Republic' is untrue. The Republic in Madrid consisted of a
Socialist and Liberal anti-clerical government. In Barcelona it was an anarcho-syndicalist Catalan nationalist
movement. In Bilbao it was the Basques. By September
1936 the rebels held much of Spain, nearly to Madrid;
by early 1937 they had occupied Malaga and much
of the Basque country. Caballero, who had been Primo
de Rivera's Minister of Labour, became Prime Minister in September 1936 and tried to organise a united

popular front, to fight the army. Since the army had
gone over to the rebels, resistance was sporadic and
local; the central government had little power to order
things to be done. It had to cajole. Above all, it needed
arms; Caballero sought them from abroad. Germany
and Italy supported Franco and the generals. The
Soviet Union began to send some aid to the government. To stop the fight between fascism and communism being enacted through Spain, Blum, the French
Socialist Prime Minister, appealed for a policy of non-
intervention by all governments, especially not to
supply arms. Britain, France, Germany, Italy, the
Soviet Union and Portugal were among the twenty-
seven nations that signed the Non-Intervention Pact.
In fact, since Franco had the army, this was a heavily
anti-government act. It was made more so by the fact
that Italy sent armies to fight for Franco, and the Germans sent a considerable quantity of arms, especially
planes and munitions. They also blockaded the Spanish
ports so that the government could get few if any
arms.

Socialists and democrats throughout Europe thought
they saw a militaristic, mostly fascist regime of immense beastliness fighting and defeating genuine workers' armies, unquestionably led by brave socialists,
anarchists and democrats. The propaganda against
fascism was enormous; some young men went and
fought in the International Brigade. What was less
clearly seen was that the communists were increasingly
taking over the republican fight and that (as in Yugoslavia six years later) at least as much of their effort
went into destroying socialists, anarchists and Catalan
nationalists as in fighting the fascists. These people
were denounced as Trotskyists, since it was the height
of the Stalin terror in Russia. Thus in Barcelona, at the
time of the greatest Basque struggle, there was a bitter
fight between the anarchists and the communists. The
communists seized the opportunity to demand central
control of the war – which meant their taking control –
and Largo Caballero fell from office, to be replaced by
Negrín.

Gradually, in one heroic battle after another, the
non-fascists were defeated, until by February 1939
Franco was victorious. The republican leaders fled.

Their supporters were imprisoned and murdered by the hundred thousand, and refugees were herded into camps on the French frontier.

What the world saw was that a Socialist government had been attacked by the fascists who had been supported by the army, the Church, the landowners and the business classes. Fascists from Germany and Italy had sent massive support. Right-wing governments elsewhere had boycotted the Republic and had established the conditions by which it was bound to fail to equip its army. The people of Spain had nevertheless fought heroically, assisted by foreign comrades in the International Brigade. What the world did not see was that the republican front had been a congeries of factions and that the communists had behaved ruthlessly towards their rivals. They saw the Soviet Union as a major supporter of the Popular-Front government and not as a vindictive partisan of Stalinism against other left-wing parties.

In 1939 came the Nazi-Soviet pact. For two years Hitler and Stalin were allies, but after Hitler's invasion of Russia in June 1941 this period was forgotten. The rise of resistance movements to Hitler's occupied Europe recreated the Spanish War: as had been the case in Spain, the resistance fought an unorthodox guerrilla war and did so as part of a Popular Front, including all anti-fascist elements and especially the communists.

The Spanish Civil War thus showed socialists that unity with the communists was possible. It showed informed socialists, like Orwell and the Labour Party, that such unity could be used by the communists to take over a popular front. It showed uninformed socialists that the only defence against fascist capitalism was a popular front.

## Wartime

When the Germans and Russians invaded Poland in 1939, and the Russians invaded Finland a little later, the long-threatened war broke out. The communists denounced the war as a capitalist conspiracy, and in the occupied areas of Poland and Finland the social democrats were among the first to be arrested. Thus, though Hitler's regime was evil and his aggression beyond reasonable doubt, for a considerable part of the left the war did not at first have an ideological content. This absence of ideology was partly explained by the absence of war – a virtual lull until April 1940, so that it seemed to many people that it was just the First World War resumed, a matter for generals and Foreign Offices. In ten weeks, between early April and later June, 1940, however, the whole context changed. The Germans occupied Denmark, Norway, Holland, Belgium and France. Italy came into the war. All the countries occupied were liberal democracies, several of them with Social Democratic governments. The war changed its character overnight. It seemed as though the fascist countries, with the tacit support of the communists and the Soviet Union, would conquer all Europe. Social democrats like Blum were among those early arrested.

In Britain, the Labour Party rallied to the defence of the country, and was instrumental in arranging for the resignation of the conservative Prime Minister, Chamberlain (branded as 'the man of Munich', whom all parties had applauded vigorously only twenty months before), and the succession to his office of Winston Churchill. Thereafter, for a year, the British fought the Germans and Italians virtually alone. The communist newspaper *The Daily Worker* was banned because of its pro-German sympathies but, such people apart, the country was virtually united in its opposition to the Axis powers. The war went badly, despite the British victory in the Battle of Britain. In early 1941 the Balkans were lost and there were defeats in North Africa. The sea war (the Battle of the Atlantic) was almost lost, too.

This period of the war was of great importance for social democracy. In Europe resistance was organised by social democrats and liberals, with communist opposition. The later version that was put about, that the communists organised the resistance, was wholly untrue. In Britain, the Labour Party took some of the most prominent departments and was largely responsible for domestic policy – Ernest Bevin at the Ministry of Labour, Herbert Morrison at the Home Office, and Clement Attlee as Deputy Prime Minister. In the process they and their colleagues, and the temporary civil servants who came in with the new government, invented what was to be known as the welfare state. British industry was also wholly taken over by government regulation.

The process was an important one because the Labour government elected in 1945 adopted the whole wartime pattern of government intervention as its own, and what happened in the war was largely identified as social democracy. Virtually all the resources of the country were devoted to a common purpose. If the purpose were peaceful, it was argued, then all social and economic problems could easily be solved. The fact that all the national resources could be used depended on a remarkable spirit of national unity: the wartime coalition government was a genuine coalition and not a 'National' government, as the government of 1931–40 had been, which was predominantly Conservative. The national unity rested upon a principle of conscription of property and manpower: few, if any,

Socialists played a prominent part in the European resistance movement. French poster of 1946: 'Yesterday, under the German occupation our socialist militants fought without respite in the underground struggle against Nazi oppression'

HIER

SOUS L'OCCUPATION ALLEMANDE

LE POPULAIRE

DANS LA CLANDESTINITÉ NOS MILITANTS SOCIALISTES ONT LUTTÉ SANS RELACHE CONTRE L'OPPRESSION NAZIE

Londoners sleeping in the Underground during an air-raid. The war forced upon the British a sense of pulling together which later socialist governments never succeeded in reproducing

individual rights were regarded as absolute. Yet at the same time a remarkable degree of freedom of expression was guaranteed. Allied to this was a sharp reduction in poverty, and a rise in living standards of the manual working class, associated with full employment, improved welfare benefits, price control, and food rationing. Public expenditure rose to unprecedented heights, without catastrophe, and many ordinary people felt better off. There was, too, an Owenite simplicity of life and thought that was sedulously encouraged by the radio and by the films and press. It seemed like an ideal socialist state – plain living, high thinking, fairly prosperous, united, well groomed and reasonably free. The British entered into a period of well justified self-congratulation which was to become the Labour Party's substitute for an ideology.

The disasters of the war, which were compensated for by the sense of being the only nation that was actually fighting Hitler, were intensified by the German invasion of its ally, Russia, in June 1941. The German armies conquered the whole of the Ukraine, the Baltic republics, and White Russia, parts of the Caucasus, and invaded Russia itself. Had Hitler not been so utterly xenophobic it is possible that the republics that were occupied would have welcomed him as a liberator. Large parts of the population undoubtedly did so, until his occupying forces showed themselves to be as brutal as the Stalinists. The immediate effect of the invasion

of the Soviet Union, however, was to switch communist propaganda to a tremendous attack on Hitler and
whole-hearted support for the war. In December 1941
the Japanese attacked Pearl Harbor and the war became virtually world-wide. Until the end of 1942, after
the victories of El Alamein in Egypt, of Stalingrad
and of the Midway Sea, it looked as though Germany,
Italy and Japan were winning. Thereafter, slowly
through 1943, and with ever-growing speed through
1944, the victory of the Allied Powers was assured.
Strange allies: the increasingly social democratic British
government, headed by the anachronistic but brilliant
Churchill, the New Deal American government,
headed by the ageing Roosevelt, and communist Russia, headed by a tyrant, Stalin, whose excesses were at
least as bad as Hitler's, and possibly, in terms of the
numbers he killed and his long-term consequences,
worse.

In Europe the Underground was increasingly
penetrated by the communists and in countries like
Yugoslavia and Greece a great deal of the fighting was
between communists and non-communists, rather
than against the Germans. This produced fundamental
problems later, because the social democrats were
identified by communist propaganda as pro-fascist,
even on occasion pro-Hitler. In France and Italy, on
the other hand, 'popular front' liberation movements
developed. Again, the communists for the most part
seized control, and the social democrats were to be
placed in the awkward position of having to assert
themselves against the communists, which (objectively
speaking) would mean that they would be forced to
choose the anti-communist side. This side would have
in it elements that remained pro-Nazi, which after June
1941 was something that drove the communists to
frenzy.

From 1943 onwards, the leadership of the European
social democratic movement was seized by the British
Labour Party. The Swedes were neutral and so their
influence was negligible. The British Labour Party
was winning the war and intended to win the
peace. Retrospectively, this represented an immensely
formative period.

In foreign policy, Labour was in favour of granting

independence to India and of positive colonial development policies in Africa that might, in two or three generations, lead to African independence. European socialists were thus committed, morally, to colonial development towards independence. This was to put the French socialists into difficulties over Algeria, for the British had few territories in their possession where there were large numbers of white settlers, of some generations' standing, in the midst of an indigenous population. Labour thus fervently supported the idea of the United Nations, which, in contrast to the League of Nations, was to have power to maintain peace. Its power depended on the unity of America and Russia. This unity, which occasionally took the form of ganging-up against Churchill, was strengthened by Roosevelt's optimism about Stalin. But a curious role, which was pure fantasy, was evolved for Britain by the social democrats. Labour, it was held, was ideologically half American and half Russian. Socialism implied collectivism economically, as in Russia, and liberalism politically, as in America. Britain would thus be the honest broker. It could also interpret the world to the two great continental empires of America and Russia, because the British were a 'sea people', with contacts, through their Commonwealth (as the Empire had become), with all races and all places. This lunatic notion, totally disregarding the reality of Russia's tyranny, of Britain's weakness and total involvement in the future of the United States, became the dominant motif of social democratic theorists, the basis of the Common Market (rapidly captured by French technocrats and German industrialists), and the ostensible reason for the attacks on Bevin's postwar foreign policy of forging links with the United States.

Domestically, Labour favoured the continuation of wartime economic controls, except over labour, and the extension of public authority by nationalising coal, electricity, gas, transport and steel (the so-called 'basic' industries). Especially it was in favour of bulk purchase of imports, bulk purchase agreements on trade with other countries, and the continuation of food and raw materials rationing. The major landmark was the adoption by the government and the Treasury of Keynes's economic policies. A government statement on full employment endorsed the principle of maintaining the level of demand by fiscal action, including unbalanced budgets. Thus Labour's policy was one of high taxation, using the budget as an economic regulator, low interest rates (the war was financed at 3 per cent) and physical controls over many aspects of economic life.

Socially, the coalition government accepted the Beveridge scheme of social insurance, designed to end the Poor Law, and the conception of a National Health Service, and it initiated in the Education Act of 1944 a major programme of educational reform. Thus Labour's domestic social policy was almost all derived from the war. It was later to be shown that the wartime dislocations had only been acceptable because of the response of public authorities in actively coping with the resulting personal crises. For example, the hospital services were nationalised in the war, to cope with air-raid casualties, and it would have been impossible to unscramble them at the end of the war. The social security system had to deal generously, quickly and efficiently with the wives and children of men at war, with evacuees, and with innumerable other cases. A return to pre-war attitudes was impossible.

When the war ended, the impression was widespread that it had been won by 'social democracy' in action.

1944 cartoon of the Beveridge Scheme from the pro-Labour newspaper the *Daily Herald*. In his report which first appeared in 1942 Sir William Beveridge recommended a thorough recasting of the social services, the adoption of a system of children's allowances, an all-in health service and a constructive government policy of 'full employment' along Keynesian lines

# Peace and the Cold War

## The Labour victory and European Socialism

The leader of the Labour Party, Clement Attlee, campaigning during the elections of 1951

On 26 July 1945 the results of the election held three weeks earlier became known in Britain. For the first time Labour had won an overwhelming electoral victory – 365 seats – though less than half the total votes cast. It was probably the biggest boost that social democracy had ever had. The great war leader, Churchill, was dismissed. A clean break with the past was indicated. Wartime socialism was to be used to win the peace.

Throughout Europe a similar pattern showed itself. Social democrats were in office in Scandinavia. They entered governments in France, Italy, Belgium, Holland, Czechoslovakia, and in other Eastern European states. Labour, as the government of the leading victorious country of Europe, was the leader of what looked like an international tide.

Its initial policies were clear. In important respects they were never changed. The 'rethinking' of the 1950s was a revision of an orthodoxy that was established in 1945; and that orthodoxy was an endorsement of wartime policies. (Socialism, not diplomacy, now became war by other means.) The Labour Party's first job was demobilisation. This demobilisation took an astonishingly long time – over a year longer than in the United States – allegedly because of a shortage of shipping, but in reality because 'fairness' dominated everything. A scheme was worked out by which a combination of age and length of service released people from the armed forces. Fairness was more important than speed. This preoccupation with fairness ran through many Labour policies. Rationing of food, clothes, raw materials, petrol, and some other commodities was maintained, often at lower than wartime levels and at considerable sacrifice of consumer satisfaction, because it was 'fair'. In Europe, on the other hand, rationing broke down, both because there was a large agricultural population who ate and sold as they liked, and because, in the war, to evade regulations was the mark of a patriot.

An additional reason for slow demobilisation was the fear of a slump. After a brief boom, the First World War had been followed by an acute depression as wartime demand fell off; a similar reaction was expected in 1946. In fact the opposite occurred. The pent-up

Conservative poster of 1959. The Labour government of 1945–51 became inextricably associated in many people's minds with post-war rationing as it struggled to be 'fair' to all

demand for goods was enormous. It was added to by
the collapse of the continental European economy –
aid had to be given to Germany and to some of the
allied countries. A world dollar shortage developed.
British and European exports had collapsed. The United States and Canada became the major suppliers of
food, raw materials and manufactured goods. A major
loan from the United States and Canada was negotiated
for Britain. A condition of the loan was free convertibility of the pound and dollar in mid-1947. This was
a critical decision. Not only did it tie the British economy irrevocably to that of the United States but it
made clear that the nature of the tie was to be on the
basis of the Bretton Woods agreements on the expansion of world trade. The socialist arguments for bulk
trading agreements between governments and for a
tightly controlled autarchic economy were doomed.
Since Eastern Europe was forced by the Soviet Union
to adopt this path, the Iron Curtain was created by
different international trading procedures. This determination of the trade pattern was endorsed by the
Marshall Plan which, though available to Eastern
European countries, was rejected by them on Russian
orders.

Economically, then, the trading arrangements adopted
in 1945 and 1946 committed Britain to the restoration
of a market economy. But meanwhile the wartime
controls were perpetuated and a peacetime administrative apparatus was constructed entirely on a wartime
model. This provided a strong contrast with Europe,
where the peacetime administration (except in Scandinavia) had been run down and the wartime administration was unacceptable. Social democrats in Europe
were collaborating with communists in some cases and
liberals in others to create new institutions. These institutions could not rest upon the high degree of detailed control that was adopted in Britain because the
mechanics of government were not adapted to their
efficient functioning. The problems in Europe, were
also of a different order. In Germany and Austria, the
country was divided into four occupation zones and
the economy had collapsed. In Italy, too, the economy
had virtually collapsed. In France, the country was
functioning, but only just, and hardship was wide-

A mine in the north of
England is nationalised
in 1947

spread. In Eastern Europe there was widespread destruction and poverty.

Therefore, what Britain did seemed to continental countries to be both unattainable – an ideal – and remote from the European reality. In Europe the real question was whether the existing political system would be replaced by a Communist regime. In areas occupied by the Red Army, the Communists were dominant. In Italy and France they provided an alternative to the temporary regimes that prevailed and an alternative that might be voted in at any time. In Britain the Communist party was minute, though its influence in some trade unions was important and some of the Labour Members of Parliament were also undercover members of the Communist Party.

The Labour government initiated a programme of nationalisation. First were the Bank of England and the airlines. Then followed coal, railways and some road transport, gas and electricity. All these activities were already heavily controlled by the government, so that the immediate impact of the change was small, especially as the vesting dates (January 1947 for coal, January 1948 for the railways) were some time in the future. A similar pattern of nationalisation occurred in many European countries, where the consequences, as in Britain, were few. In France some of the banks and some manufacturing industries were included. In Italy, the state remained in the field of industrial development, using Mussolini's state finance corporation for the purpose.

Labour continued the Herbert Morrison policy of arranging the nationalised industries under state corporations, which resembled in most respects the larger privately owned corporations. There was no worker participation, as there would have been under syndicalism, and there was no consumer control, as in the co-operative movement. It followed that the vast bureaucratic organisations running big industries had few friends – the private industrialists disliked them, and the socialist organisations distrusted them. As most of the industries (except electricity) that were nationalised were making heavy losses, it was inevitable that nationalisation would very rapidly become a potent source of unpopularity for the Labour Party. Socialists were angry at the large compensation payments made to the private shareholders; taxpayers resented the losses; the workers found that the managers they worked under were the same as in private ownership. It was indeed unfortunate that immediately after the nationalisation of coal there should have been a very severe winter. The country ran out of coal, electricity supplies were cut, everyone was cold and millions were thrown temporarily out of work. Labour never really recovered from this disaster.

On the social side, Labour carried on wartime reforms which set a pattern for Europe. It was, indeed, a pattern that in many respects was improved upon by the Europeans. First, in 1946, the National Insurance and National Industrial Injury Acts were passed which, for flat-rate contributions, gave flatrate benefits to the retired, the sick and the unemployed. (Family allowances had already been instituted by the coalititon government.) Then the National Health Service Act was passed, providing a comprehensive, free medical service for the whole community, including hospitals, general practitioners, drugs, dentistry and preventive services. These Acts came into force on 5 July 1948, but already, by early 1946, they represented the hallmark of social democracy. The 'Welfare State', which provided universal free benefits in health and welfare, was opposed to the old conception of benefits only for the poor; the universality implied both equality and 'fairness' – or fraternity. To the rationing system, with everybody getting the same small quantity of meat, sugar, fats and clothes, was added equal old age pensions, equal health care, and a stab at equal housing, for the Labour government initiated a big local authority housing programme designed to provide the majority of houses in the country.

Thus by 1946 the Labour government's domestic programme was clearly outlined. Its foreign policy was already radically shifting. Labour had been elected as a mediator between capitalism (the United States) and communism. Ernest Bevin, the Foreign Secretary, maintained the Anglo-American alliance and it soon appeared evident that there was no wish on the part of the Communists to maintain the Anglo-Russian alliance. The details of this period are still obscure

but the main outline of the story appears to be that
Stalin determined to hold on to his gains in Eastern
Europe, to eliminate the Social Democrats there, and
to try to capture the countries of Western Europe not
occupied by the Red Army through internal subver-
sion. Thus in 1946 the Communists withdrew from the
French government. In Germany, four-power control
rapidly dwindled into an Eastern zone occupied by the
Red Army to which Britain and the United States had
limited access, and three Western zones that were ad-
ministered within an allied framework. The Labour
government determined 'to keep America in Europe'
at any cost, since (in their view) the Versailles Treaty
and the League of Nations had been wrecked by American non-participation. Thus, both financially and in
foreign policy, the Attlee government planned to keep
closely in step with American foreign policy and far
from Labour being an intermediary between capitalism and communism to make America and Europe the
adversaries of communism.

# Euphoria and crisis

The election of the Labour government in Britain in
1945 was the high point of social democratic euphoria.
Though many of their aims – prosperity, the substantial
elimination of poverty and wider educational opportunity – were to be achieved, they were to be achieved,
not by the introduction of socialism but by social
reform, in a world deeply divided by the issue of
communism.

Ernest Bevin's attitude to communism was affected
by two major experiences. The first was his defeat of
communist infiltration in his trade union, the Transport and General Workers Union. He had experienced
every type of conspiracy to capture the union, including practices later to be revealed in court in the
Electrical Trades Union case. Bevin's second experience was in foreign policy. The Greek communists
had captured the Resistance in Greece and had used
their success to try to overthrow the regime which had
returned with the British liberation of Greece in December 1944. A civil war broke out, with British troops
helping the non-communist government. When Bevin
continued this policy after July 1945, with clear

evidence of a communist determination to make Greece
a communist republic by any means, he was subjected
to every kind of vilification, expecially by the Communists and their allies in the Labour Party. By late
1946, with the Red Army not demobilised and with
the American troops almost all returned to the United
States, the British troops alone seemed to defend Greece
and Turkey against Communist invasion. The invasion
would no doubt have taken the form it subsequently
did in Hungary in 1956 and in Czechoslovakia in 1968,
of helping the local communists to restore order. But
the threat seemed real enough. The British government
therefore reaffirmed continually the need to defend
Europe against communism.

1946 was therefore a curious year. On the one hand
was the euphoria of victory. Rarely in modern times
had a regime been so utterly defeated as Nazi Germany
had been. The defeat had been followed by substantial
electoral victories for the socialists almost wherever
elections were held. The restoration of Europe, it
seemed, would be a rebirth – a rebirth of a socialist
Europe. The full horrors of Stalinism, which propaganda had suppressed during the war, were as yet almost unknown. The general public, and especially the
politically conscious, hoped for a rapprochement between the Socialist governments of the West and the
Communist governments of the East. Formally the
governments in Eastern Europe were coalitions, built
round a strong Communist Party, but still coalitions.
Familiar social democrats were in office, especially in
Czechoslovakia – Beneš and Masaryk – and Rumania
and Bulgaria were still monarchies with young kings.
It seemed as though all countries would become Den-
marks or Swedens, if luck held and goodwill was not
thwarted by vested interests. That was why Bevin
seemed to many to be the evil genius of socialism, for
it was he who constantly spoke out about the conditions in Eastern Europe and about the plans of the
Soviet Union to subvert and possibly to invade the
West.

Bevin seemed the odd man out. Yet in Greece the
Civil War raged. In Palestine, too, the Jews sought to
expand the area of Jewish settlement. The Arabs pro-
tested. Bevin supported the Arabs, allegedly because

The Czech foreign
minister Jan Masaryk
in the summer of 1947.
In 1948 he fell, or was
pushed, out of a
window to his death

he feared for British oil interests in Arab countries. It seemed that, despite the Labour government, the Foreign Office was exerting all its powers to exercise a non-socialist foreign policy, and that President Truman, who succeeded Roosevelt in April 1945, was swinging America into supporting British imperialism. Though it was the declared policy of Labour to give India independence, there was great difficulty in finding an agreed successor government since the Muslims and the Hindus could not agree on a unified state. Thus, internationally, it could plausibly argued that Bevin and the Labour government were deliberately preventing world peace and socialism from achieving a just triumph.

The early euphoria of economic recovery, helped everywhere by demobilisation and the overcoming of some of the more gross of the problems left by the war, was giving way to a slowing up and then a regression into chaos. Britain ran first into an acute problem of fuel supplies, which revealed the more general economic difficulty of continuous pressure of too much demand on limited resources. Underlying this difficulty was the balance of payments problem. Before the war Britain's imports had always exceeded its exports but the difference was usually made up by earnings on overseas assets. Many of these assets had been sold to finance imports during the war and very substantial debts had been built up. To meet the gap between imports and exports it was now necessary for Britain to limit imports and to step up exports. This determined the whole economic strategy of the Labour government. The pound became convertible in 1947, and within a few days the run on the reserves was so great that convertibility had to be stopped. It was, in the circumstances, impossible for Britain to adopt a 'socialist' economic policy, since imports were almost at a minimum and hope of trade with the devastated Soviet Union was illusory. A 'socialist' economic policy of high production would have required higher imports of raw materials. Many raw materials were not available and the rest could not be afforded. The European problem was a different one. The industrial structure of France, Italy and Germany was so disoriented that chronic imbalance developed. These imbalances could to some extent be overcome by imports, though with the world shortage of food and raw materials it was impossible to overcome the more desperate problems. By mid-1947 the situation looked almost hopeless. There was a growing feeling that the communists might win the Italian elections and that the big French Communist Party would be able to take over France. On the other hand, the European economic problem was different from Britain's, because once the pump had been primed, their overseas earnings position looked far more favourable.

Britain's balance of payments difficulties precipitated a solution to the problem. After the fuel crisis, the Labour government told President Truman's administration that it could no longer afford to maintain substantial forces in Greece to protect Greece and Turkey. President Truman then enunciated 'the Truman doctrine', which the communists identified as the beginning of the Cold War. This doctrine implied that the Yalta settlement could not be overthrown and that the Americans would rearm and station troops in Europe in order to prevent Soviet aggression. This dramatic reversal of American disarmament

Ernest Bevin, the British Foreign Minister, signing the Marshall Aid Charter in Paris in 1948. In his view it had 'been devised to help not only to administer American aid but also to bring about a permanently sound European economy'

represented a triumph for Ernest Bevin. His principal fear, that the Americans would withdraw from Europe as they had done in 1919, was allayed. The Americans were now involved in Europe. This meant ultimately that social democrats abandoned the notion of building a bridge between America and communism.

Some of them had abandoned the notion already. Throughout Europe, however, some social democrats allied themselves with the communists. This happened in Italy and France. A number of 'fellow-travellers' – euphemism for underground communists – were expelled from the Labour Party. Thus in France and Germany the left was predominantly communist, while in Britain, Holland and Scandinavia it was social democrat. The non-fellow-travelling social democrats (except in Sweden) were pro-American; and this meant that the pro-American splinter groups in France and Italy were allied with the growing centre parties against the left.

There had been a significant resurgence of moderate Catholic parties in Europe. After the war, with the disappearance of extreme right-wing, pro-fascist organisations, the moderates had formed parties on the basis of a religious, democratic, radical programme. The Christian Democratic Party was one such in Italy; the *Mouvement Républicain Populaire* was a similar formation in France. One simple point may be made here about these bourgeois parties. They were anti-communist. As the Cold War intensified, one of their major attractions was their anti-communism. But as the historian H. R. Trevor-Roper has remarked, before the Second World War the bourgeoisie supported fascism because it was anti-communist. These Catholic and Liberal parties were not fascist. Their ideological basis was remarkably similar to that of the Labour Party. It was anti-communist but it supported the idea of an organic community based on generous social services. In Italy and France the Christian Democratic Party and MRP were supporters of a considerable degree of government intervention in the economy. Above all, they were democrats and supported republican democratic institutions. When the social democrats allied themselves with the christian democrats, therefore, they were not (at that period) allying themselves to laissez-faire parties.

In Germany the situation was to be different. There, the Communist Party was to be both illegal and unpopular, because of its behaviour in the Soviet occupation zone, where Ulbricht, the communist dictator, was one of the worst Stalinist tyrants. The Christian Democrats became convinced supporters of laissez-faire (though initiating a very significant structure of social security). Therefore, in what was to become Western Germany, the Social Democrats were opposed to the Christian Democrats.

Thus, in Western Europe as a whole, there were parties in office which had similar views, but in France and Italy they were Christian Democrats, with moderate social democrat support, while in Britain and Scandinavia they were Social Democrats. It was this situation that caused the Communist Parties to regard the Social Democrats as lackeys of the Christian Democrats whom they saw, in turn, as American capitalist-front parties. The drift to supporting 'capitalism' was, however, a later phenomenon of christian democracy; in 1947 and 1948 its orientation was towards a Labour Party type of government, especially in the field of the social services. It was Adenauer and Erhard who, by liberating Germany from its complex system of economic controls, subsequently created the 'free enterprise' boom of the 1950s – the so-called German economic miracle – which made christian democracy pro-capitalist.

In 1947 the German economic miracle was far away. The communists were consolidating their power in Eastern Europe and it seemed as though they might gain France and Italy. An invasion of Greece seemed possible, despite the Truman doctrine. As the year wore on, economic difficulties intensified. It was in this context that the American Secretary of State, General Marshall, spoke of a recovery programme for Europe, supported by the United States but representing a co-operative multilateral effort by the European countries, including the Soviet bloc. His idea was enthusiastically endorsed by Bevin. Negotiations began. Eventually, despite a wish by Czechoslovakia and Poland to join in, the European Recovery Programme

Russian cartoon, showing NATO dancing to the tune of the United States. The economic and military dependence of post-war Western Europe on the United States was a decisive factor in shaping socialist policy

– known as the Marshall Plan – was initiated for all Western European nations. The mechanism was that the United States paid dollars into a pool in Europe. European nations also made contributions to this pool and withdrawals were made to support programmes for recovery. Thus, for a nation like Britain, the actual aid was zero; the dollars from the pool covered the dollar deficit in the British balance of payments, while the pounds put into the pool by Britain covered the other nations' pound deficits. The principal recipients of aid were Western Germany, France and Italy.

By the end of 1947, Western Europe had set out on two paths, both in close alliance with the United States. Rearmament was the first, and this was to culminate in a coordination of arms policies through the North Atlantic Treaty (NATO). The second was economic recovery through the European Recovery Programme (the Marshall Plan) which entailed a systematic dismantling of trade restrictions between European countries and between Europe and America. These two programmes set the pattern for the 1950s.

European social democracy, therefore, had to fit into a picture of increasingly close relations with the United States, both militarily and economically. It faced, too, a dramatic intensification of Stalinism in Eastern Europe. Squeezed between these two giants, far from being a bridge, social democracy became a chasm of empty ideology and failing policies. Its social and industrial policies existed on the bounty of America and its very survival depended on the American nuclear umbrella.

## The Cold War

The introduction of the Marshall Plan, and American rearmament, saved the Western economy. But 1948 was dramatic in other respects. The Cold War became a terrible reality. In Czechoslovakia the communists created a terrorist state, and with Masaryk's suicide or (more probably) murder, it was clear that no social democrat could survive in a Communist regime unless he recanted. In Hungary socialists were executed after a sham trial, and elsewhere in Eastern Europe the socialists were imprisoned, or disappeared. The Greek Civil War was virtually ended, with victory for the

monarchists. Significantly helping this victory was the fact that Yugoslavia – a supply base for Greek communist guerrilla fighters – defected from Stalin's empire. Thus, for the first time since Trotsky was expelled from the Communist party, the Stalinists split.

The Yugoslav developments followed an increasing number of defections from communism. Arthur Koestler and others published innumerable books and articles explaining why they had left the Communist party. Some became Roman Catholics or Quakers. The defections were dramatised by developments in the United States where it was revealed that a network of communists had worked for many years in the Federal government and conspired to overthrow the United States. It became an era of the unmasking of spies – the Rosenbergs and other atom spies, and Alger Hiss – leading increasingly to a strongly anti-communist spirit which reached its extreme form in Senator McCarthy's campaign against liberal democrats who had sympathised with causes that were now known to have been infiltrated by communists. Distasteful though the campaign was, it has to be said that there was evidence that communists had infiltrated many liberal organisations, though there was little evidence that they had been successful in affecting public policy as a result.

For socialists, the most significant causes of defection were given by those who claimed that Stalin had perverted communism. They drew attention to the Russian oppression of other nationalities – this was

The height of the Cold War: Slav exiles demonstrating during a 'loyalty day' parade on Fifth Avenue, New York. These parades were dedicated to the ideal that 'loyalty means liberty' and were led by eminent

primarily the cause of Tito's Yugoslavia's break with Stalin. They spoke of the terrible tyranny in Russia – the shooting and exiling of millions of people, of the purges and the Stalin terror, of the incredibly arbitrary nature of Soviet rule. Above all, Stalin threatened the world with a renewed war. He was a man for whom little could be said.

His acolytes, who were many, said a lot: they denied that Stalin had aggressive intentions, despite the clear evidence of Czechoslovakia. That they explained away by saying that the Czechs wanted it and that Stalin was forestalling an American move to 'liberate' Eastern Europe. They denied that there were persecutions in Russia. They denied that there was anti-semitism.

The socialists who were deceived were many, and they were chiefly to be found in countries with large Communist Parties. The social democrats proper re-affirmed their belief in democratic, constitutional, representative government. They aligned themselves with America. Two things then occurred that were important. The first was the siege of Berlin – a four-power zone in the midst of Soviet-occupied Germany – by the Soviet occupation forces. It was decided by the American, British and French governments to run an airlift into Berlin. This was done. It dramatised both the threat of communism and the military response that was necessary to deal with it. The immediate cause of the siege was the establishment of the German Federal Republic in 1948, to cover the three Western occupation zones. In the general election the Christian Democratic Party gained a major victory, with the Social Democrats as the opposition. This victory re-presented the beginning of a major electoral recession of social democracy throughout the West. It was followed by a dramatic improvement in the German economic performance and by a steady diminution in the reputation and standing of Social Democratic Parties.

The year 1948 marked, then, a major development in the Cold War – the organisation of the West around America, both for defence and for economics. President Truman, to everybody's astonishment, was re-elected in 1948, but America had decisively shifted its position towards militant anti-communism. It had shifted be-cause of China (where the communists were in the

process of driving Chiang Kai Shek, America's ally, off
the mainland), because of Berlin, because of what was
happening in Eastern Europe, because of spies within –
because it all added up to a threat that the Soviet Union
was about to embark on an aggressive war to conquer
all Europe, as China was being conquered. Voices were
raised to suggest a pre-emptive atomic war against the
Soviet Union. Bertrand Russell was one of those who
held that it was highly necessary to defeat communism,
at almost any cost, before communism had the power
and the ability to send atomic bombs to the west.

In this situation, the choices were agonising for socialists. Should they support the tyrannies of Russia or
the capitalists of America? Book after book tumbled
into the bookshops arguing that the Soviet Union need
not necessarily have gone sour. It was due to Stalin.
Stalin, in turn, was due to the isolation of the Soviet
Union, beginning with allied intervention in favour
of the Whites in 1919, followed by the *cordon sani-
taire*, followed by the postwar Anglo-American
alliance. This highly selective reading of history, which
ignored the Comintern, the Nazi-Soviet pact, and the
occupation of Europe east of the Elbe by the Red
Army, made a great impression, especially in Yugoslavia and India.

India was emerging as the light of the East. In 1947
the British had withdrawn from the Indian Empire and
two successor states had been established – India and
Pakistan – whose inhabitants had fallen upon each other
with terrifying ferocity. More than a million people
were killed in less than a month. After this slaughter,
India set itself up as a sanctimonious, secular, socialist
state, led by Pandit Nehru. Its brand of socialism owed
a great deal to that incompatible trio Tolstoy and the
Webbs. Gandhi was an old-fashioned, Tolstoyan,
vegetarian pacifist. He was convinced – and others were
too – that India had become independent of the British
because passive resistance had driven them out. This
happened, unfortunately, not to be true. They had
withdrawn because they were bankrupt and could not
afford an army to occupy India, because of American
pressure, and because the Labour Party sincerely believed in self-determination. Yet Gandhi, who was
almost immediately assassinated, started a myth, which

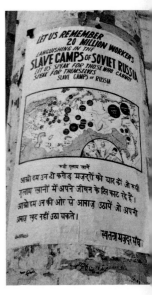

A Mayday poster in
New Delhi in 1955.
The Indian Congress
Party's pursuit of a
socialist-orientated
form of government
within a democratic
framework was held
up by European social
democrats as a model
for the Third World

was to be very potent, that passive resistance would be more successful than armed resistance to invasion. If this were so, then the Cold War could be fought with spiritual and costless weapons.

Thus, India, home of passive resistance, became a socialist Mecca. Its role, taken over from the British Labour Party of 1945, was to be a bridge between communism and capitalism. A great many left-wing economists were hired to draw up innumerable and conflicting plans for industrial development, agricultural improvement, educational advance, taxation reform, expropriation of the rich and endowment of the poor, birth control and health reform. The bureaucracy swelled to an enormous size. As Gunnar Myrdal, one of the most enthusiastic advisers, was to point out in 1968, nothing happened. Mother India continued unchanged, traditional to the last, and defeated in war by the Chinese and the Pakistanis. But in 1949 socialist euphoria was at its height; the only regret was that the Webbs were dead. They would have loved it.

George Orwell broadcasting from the BBC in 1942. From left to right (standing) are George Woodcock, Mulk Raj Anand, Orwell, William Empson and (seated) Herbert Read and Edmund Blunden

George Orwell was one of those who, faced with the reality of Stalinism in the Spanish Civil War in 1937, had chosen democracy. His view hardened as the Second World War developed and pro-Soviet propaganda became dominant on the left. Modern technology and the absence of any moral restraints had given a socialist state total power over its inhabitants. Not only could they be thrown in gaol, tortured, and executed, as they had been in Germany, Italy and Russia, but their very existence could be denied. History could be rewritten, as Soviet history was rewritten to exclude Trotsky and other unpersons. People could only live, work, marry and have children by permission of the state and the Party. Unlike medieval Catholicism or other earlier tyrannies, the twentieth century was yielding to a tyranny of a drab industrial kind with no redeeming features. Its art was despicable; its social tone typified by the ration card, the queue, the overall as a uniform, the factory with its endless canned music, mass recreation. In such a society, the very ideals of socialism – of diversity and equality, of freedom and fraternity – were meaningless. His two books – *Animal Farm* and *1984* – enunciating his view of the Soviet horror, were the authentic voice of English socialism. Yet the alternative, an enthusiastic prosecution of the Cold War, seemed to imply a wholesale adoption of Americanism. America which, periodically, had been the Golden Land of the left – especially under Roosevelt – had now become a McCarthyite ogre.

Yet it had to be admitted that it seemed as though capitalism was overtaking social democracy. While Britain was rationed and poor, Belgium had recovered without rationing. Travellers' tales of steaks, silk stockings and American cars brought sneers to the lips of the English, accustomed to look upon Belgium as a Breughelesque mixture of vulgar hedonism and working-class neglect. But the German economic miracle was beginning to work. Despite the Marshall Plan, the British economy faltered; in 1949 a major devaluation was necessary. Rationing continued for years after the end of the war. In early 1950 the Labour government was re-elected, but with a tiny margin of a majority. It looked as if the end of social democracy was at hand Europe, far from copying the Labour government, as seemed probable in 1945, was reviving under American guidance and with free enterprise.

A major philosophical shift was occurring. Though the Labour Party had identified itself with rationing, detailed control of the economy, and fair shares, its theorists had argued that the duty of a social democratic government was to ensure full employment and an equitable distribution of the national income. Thereafter the price mechanism would ensure that consumers' satisfaction was maximised. This thesis, advanced in the 1930s by Abba Lerner, was now proposed in Britain by James Meade and Arthur Lewis. A more confused writer, Barbara Wootton, had advocated 'planning'. But planning had been identified with detailed bureaucratic control; an alternative was a long-term strategic view of the economy. But this long-term view was tarnished by the echo of the Soviet Five-Year Plan. There seemed no middle way. *The Economist* newspaper, edited by Geoffrey Crowther, advocated an alternative – maintain full employment and let the economy rip. But full employment should be defined as rather more men competing for rather fewer jobs. In contrast, then, to the socialist price theorists, Crowther would have maintained as 'full employment' what would have entailed a degree of unemployment which was unacceptable to the Labour government and the trade unions. To adopt this policy, however, seemed to lead to two difficulties – an internal level of demand that caused the threat of continually rising prices and wages, and a pressure of demand that continually drew in imports at a higher level than export earnings could finance. Both tendencies, the price rise and the import propensity, were contained only by severe physical controls over the economy. These controls included a prices and wages freeze, rationing, raw material allocation, and a paraphernalia of controls that were increasingly avoided and were increasingly arbitrary and inefficient. 'Set the people free' became a powerful slogan which was offset by the fear that if Labour left office, mass unemployment would return and the welfare state (especially the National Health Service) would be dismantled.

The Labour Chancellors of the Exchequer – Sir Stafford Cripps and Hugh Gaitskell – adopted a version

of Keynesian control of the economy that had two
defects; it did not work and it was electorally unpopular.
If the total demand on resources was estimated to ex-
ceed the resources available, then the budget surplus
was used to deflate the economy. Since the total demands in the economy continually exceeded the available resources, taxes were always being put up. There
was a steady rise in output but the rise was masked by
continually increasing taxes. As Europe became more
prosperous it seemed ironical that one of the victors
should still have rationing while in the rest of Western
Europe petrol, food, and other goods should be freely
available. The situation was worsened, in 1950, by the
outbreak of the Korean War.

The American and British governments undertook
vast rearmament programmes, the first effect of which
was a rapid rise of prices of primary goods, which
adversely affected Britain's import bill. The second
effect was a big increase in public expenditure for defence. This led to a further Gaitskell budget to raise
taxes and a cutback in welfare services. It seemed as
though the Cold War had not only led to a postpone-
ment of Elysium; it was now leading to a dismantling
of the welfare state.

At this point the leading representative of the left
wing of the Labour Party, Aneurin Bevan, who had
been Minister of Health, resigned, together with two
acolytes – Wilson (later to become Prime Minister)
and Freeman (to be given various diplomatic appoint-
ments by his co-resigner). Cripps and Bevin died. The
Labour government dithered on until, in October 1951,
it was narrowly defeated at the polls by Winston
Churchill and the Conservatives.

Thus, Western European socialism lost its leading
socialist government. Its achievements were solid – full
employment, a welfare state, a move out of empire and
a Western Alliance. But other European countries,
notably Germany, achieved all these without a reputation for sanctimonious austerity and mindless bureaucratic controls. And it rapidly became apparent that
Labour, by keeping Britain out of a European federation
and involving it in enormous military programmes,
had left a legacy which was to handicap the country
for at least twenty years.

# Rethinking

## Gaitskell and the Socialist International

The Labour government's narrow defeat in the 1951 general election marked the end of the wartime brand of social democracy. The era of world shortages of food and raw materials was almost over. The Cold War was a well-established fact. In a significant sense, the wartime socialist high tide had receded. Adenauer and the Christian Democrats were in office in Western Germany and the *Weltwirtschaftswunder* was underway; economic miracles led to a reassessment of capitalism in its new and successful form.

There were several aspects of society in the 1950s that called into question not only wartime socialism but the very concept of democratic socialism itself. There was, first of all, the problem of the Soviet Union. Despite the persistent tendency of people on the left to blame the 'capitalist' powers – especially America – for everything, the undeniable horror of Stalin's Russia became daily more apparent. There was tyranny in Eastern Europe, followed by the violent crushing of the Hungarian revolt in 1956 by the Soviet armed forces. Krushchev's speech at the Twentieth Congress of the Soviet Communist Party revealed that even communists knew of Stalin's tyranny. And there were good reasons for believing that in essentials Russian communism had not changed. On the other hand, from about 1958 to 1967 there were signs of a 'thaw', both internally and externally. And, in addition, the first Russian spacecraft, Sputnik, suggested that authoritarianism of a Soviet kind was compatible with high technological and possibly scientific achievement. The split with Yugoslavia in 1948 and with China later, suggested that communism was becoming far less monolithic; the suggestion even developed that, as Soviet society 'matured', it would become far more like the technocratic, military, capitalist society of North America. Since socialism defined itself by reference to communism, a change – whether actual or perceived – in the nature of communism meant a change in the

**Above:** The Cold War doubtless contributed to Labour's defeat in the elections of 1951: Conservative poster of 1950 exploiting curent fears of Communism.
**Opposite:** An agent of the Hungarian Security police lynched in the streets of Budapest during the short lived Hungarian uprising of 1956. Its brutality revealed the horrors of Soviet communism for all to see

nature of socialism. It would be held, for example, that, though socialism should take steps to prevent the emergence of a Stalin, it should also try to see that a Sputnik should be produced. Could democratic socialism create the conditions for massive nuclear weapons, for interplanetary flight, for the hideously expensive investment needed to rival Russia's technico-military achievements?

The second aspect of society in the 1950s that was important was the transformation of the United States. The election of General Eisenhower as President in 1952 and his appointment of John Foster Dulles as his Secretary of State led to a phase of militant, verbal anti-communism, which seemed to confirm the switch of America's posture from the left of world politics to the far right – a militant defender of capitalism that was prepared to use and to maintain right-wing authoritarian regimes in office in order to stop communism. Thus socialism, far from adopting the American posture on world affairs as it had tended to do in Roosevelt's time, was tempted to define itself as a more moderate alternative to communism.

This was most obviously seen in the Third World of the developing countries. India and Pakistan became independent in 1947; Ceylon and Burma followed; then the Middle East. In the mid-1950s this independence movement spread to Africa. Through the United Nations and regional organisations the Third World declared itself to be 'non-aligned', neither pro-Russian nor pro-American. Its acceptance of quantities of American aid, and of lesser amounts from the Soviet Union, represented no ideological commitment; it was the payment, rather, of conscience money by the rich to the poor. Since Dulles was in the habit of claiming that everyone who was not for him was against him, this had the effect of making the Third World seem pro-Soviet, especially when, as in Africa, the metropolitan country (in that case France) waged war against the insurgents. It was in the American interest to support its NATO allies; it became, therefore, simple propaganda for the Soviet Union to support the nationalists. In addition to this identification of the nationalist cause with the anti-Western cause, another factor had to be taken into account. Countries as diverse in social struc-

Opposite: The post-war Italian socialist movement has been split on the issue of what attitude to take to Moscow. While Saragat's *Partito Socialista Unitario* (PSU) collaborated in successive governments with the Christian Democrats, Pietro Nenni **(bottom)** here addressing the 25th Congress of his *Partito Socialista Italiano* (PSI) – maintained an uncompromising Marxist line

ture, religion and economic development as India,
Egypt and Indonesia declared themselves to be socialist
countries. This socialism of the Third World involved
nationalism, strong central government, a high degree
of economic planning, and (in principle) the expropriation of the large landowners and industrialists. In all
these countries the problems of the landless peasantry
loomed large, and socialism came increasingly to be
defined as a conscious attempt, by use of the state, to
improve the conditions of the rural poor. This also
involved an attack on international companies, often
of American or British origin, which appeared to
dominate particular areas of the country or sectors of
the economy, or to monopolise foreign trade.

'Right wing' socialists like Gaitskell inclined more
towards America and became violently anti-communist
while 'left-wing' socialists like Nenni inclined violently
against America and more towards the Russians. Socialists therefore were forced to react to the Cold War,
aligning increasingly with the concerns of the socialist
Third World, and especially with the Prime Minister
of India, Pandit Nehru. Socialism came to mean the
development of international institutions which would

**Below:** Saragat, the leading Italian social democrat in 1948.

reallocate world resources to ensure the rapid growth of the economies of the poor countries. It meant, increasingly, the struggle for colonial freedom and for racial equality. Racial discrimination in the United States, apartheid in South Africa, the struggle in Algeria and Vietnam – all these became symbols which were socialist symbols, as the Spanish Republican cause had once been.

But perhaps the most profound effect on socialism was that caused by full employment and rapid economic growth in Western Europe and North America. The rates of growth of the German, Italian and French economies were without precedent. Japan, with growth rates occasionally reaching 9 per cent a year, was outstanding. Even Great Britain and the United States achieved growth rates that were remarkably high compared with earlier periods. National incomes per head doubled over periods of ten to fifteen years. World trade grew even faster. This was achieved in economies that were neither capitalist, in the laissez-faire sense, nor socialist in the Moscow sense. They had big welfare budgets. France especially had a national planning system. They sought to achieve full employment, generally speaking, by fiscal and monetary means (though both Germany and the United States eschewed unbalanced budgets). International machinery was created to make world trade flow as freely and smoothly as possible. Big companies and nationalised corporations worked side by side, and in terms of management and labour relations were indistinguishable. The firms, the state and the trade unions seemed to collaborate and not to fight.

Two important books defined the new society – Andrew Shonfield's *Modern Capitalism* and J. K. Galbraith's *The Affluent Society*. Both made the point that the socialist diagnosis of capitalism was no longer relevant. Whatever it was, modern capitalism was not a society that waged imperialist war within itself. It did not impoverish the working class. It did not run into constant problems of unemployment and misery. On the contrary, it led to rapid economic growth and mounting prosperity; the very existence of the social services depended on prosperity.

The socialist case could not rely, therefore, on the

grounds that common ownership of the means of production, distribution and exchange was necessary for prosperity. The communist countries, on the contrary, where nationalisation prevailed, were drab and impoverished: a modern industrial power like Czechoslovakia had clearly slipped back since it was taken over by the communists. Gaitskell, therefore, who succeeded Attlee as leader of the Labour Party in 1955, sought unsuccessfully to make it drop its vestigial socialist commitment to this kind of economic policy. The German Social Democratic Party dropped its commitment. The Socialist International – the meeting

1959 Labour Party election poster. Gaitskell *(left)* shown with Barbara Castle and Aneurin Bevan wanted to make use of the influence of western capitalism to build a just society

LET'S HAVE A BETTER BRITAIN

VOTE LABOUR

of social democratic parties – sought to redefine socialism.

It did so in terms of the struggle for social and radical equality, the desire for peace and the desire to build up the public outlays on health, education, welfare, and the environment, to use the affluence of modern industrialism to create a more adequate and satisfying life.

It is this thesis – which was the Gaitskell thesis – that was to be adopted as the main socialist theme. Its inadequacy, the 1960s would reveal. That its philosophy was the only one for civilised men could hardly be doubted. Its practice was, however, on occasion another matter.

## Equality and poverty

Socialism meant equality, so Crosland and others held, after the process of revisionism had gone far enough to cast doubt upon public ownership of the means of production, distribution and exchange as the basis of socialism. What were the causes of inequality and, more pragmatically, what were to be the means of moving the world towards greater equality? Those were the socialist questions.

Inequality had many dimensions. It could be inequality between races, between sexes or between generations. It could be inequality of status, as between slave, serf and freeman. It could be inequality of incomes, or inequality of capital, or inequality of social status. Thus it had to be defined and measured before it could be explained. For this measurement and assessment Crosland turned to the social sciences.

The social sciences had an important role in socialist theory and practice. The earliest socialists, from Proudhon, Marx and Comte onwards, claimed that their socialism was 'scientific' – that is, that their analysis of the course of events was objectively true and corresponded to scientific criteria of observation and analysis. But a new group of sciences – calling themselves social sciences – grew up, with economics and psychology as the prime examples. To Marxists these were not sciences at all, but apologias for bourgeois society.

Socialists differed from Marxists in accepting the

Anthony Crossland, the leading British post-war socialist thinker, used his knowledge of economics to reconstruct socialist theory

methodology of the social sciences, whether in economics, psychology, sociology, social anthropology or statistics. The methodology was rooted in statistical and mathematical techniques, with emphasis upon accurate observation and upon the importance of the validation of prediction. In the course of the development of these 'scientific' social sciences, the place of social and political philosophy, of moral and aesthetic judgement, tended increasingly to be cast as mere value judgements. The implication was that the social sciences were neutral tools for discerning the truth, that judgements about society were matters of individual choice, which could not be objectively discussed and which were, indeed, often mere rhetoric.

If socialism were scientific, therefore, it implied an acceptance not only of the methodology but of the findings of the social sciences. If Marx predicted increasing mass unemployment in capitalist economies, and Keynes explained what caused mass unemployment, then Keynes's work was more socialist – because more scientific – than Marx's. Marx became merely another exploded scientist, whose tomb was erected on the long highway of scientific truth. Socialism thus became identified with social engineering; the manipulation of society, on the analogy of engineering, to attain given results. But what results? How were the targets to be set?

One appealing answer lay in the argument that certain values – truth, justice, kindness, compassion – were implicit in certain modes of life, and that the patient unravelling of complex social problems would enable difficulties to be worked through in detail, which would enable people to contain social evil. It would be hard to deny that in many respects life had become more tolerable because of patient investigation: that pedagogy, medicine, penology, for example, were immeasurably more effective and more humane because of the application of scientific methods. The use of general statements – such as that 'human nature will never alter' – was purposeless, because such assertions could only be understood in particular contexts, when they would be seen to be absurd. The patient, step-by-step approach to social questions was a way to enlarge the area of human choice, since it made what happened to people more open to rational discussion. In such a context, steps toward more equality, or towards greater social justice were not part of some grandiose scheme for human improvement, but rational choices, dictated by humane criteria, in highly specific contexts. Often, desirable aims would be in conflict and it would be necessary to trade off gains in one direction against losses in another.

The question for socialists, then, was not so much the ends as the means. The ends – equality, justice, freedom – resolved themselves (in the detail of any situation) into the humane alternative. Did the totality of these choices add up to a consistent pattern of social action, involving the use of the power of the state, that might be called socialism?

The sociologist Richard Titmuss would have answered the question affirmatively. Because the problems showed a consistent pattern, it was almost axiomatic that solutions to the problems would show a consistent pattern of response.

What was the consistency of the problems? It seemed that study of the problems of poverty and deprivation suggested that growing national incomes – the economics of affluence – created distress at a rate possibly as fast as it was alleviated, distress which was different in form but similar in nature. It was as though industrial society had a centrifugal tendency; as development took place, those at a disadvantage were flung out and fell through society to the bottom. In industrial societies there were the elderly, the mentally and physically handicapped, oppressed minority groups like Negroes, widows, children from large families and all those, who because they owned no capital and could not earn very much, if anything, became the 'poor' – the absolutely and relatively deprived. Further, as change accelerated, the number of victims of change increased; there was, thus, a constant tendency for the number of deprived people to increase. Thus inequality could be seen as a function of change. Change itself – industrialisation and automation – acting within the social context of bourgeois institutions, thus became the systematic cause of inequality, suffering and injustice.

The response to these problems was a growing network of publicly-provided social services. In the first place there was a growing political pressure from the underprivileged for the redress of their ills. There was also a growing body of professional opinion that wished to exercise its skills free from the pressures of the market place – doctors, teachers, social workers – and whose professional judgments involved radical reallocations of resources. To deal with an accident victim, for example, many thousands of dollars worth of medical skills would be needed, and then he and his family might need social security payments for many years, rehousing and other social provisions. Whether the accident was incurred in war, or in employment, on the roads, or at home, might affect his legal status as a claimant of insurance benefits but his social needs were the same. Only the state, it was argued, could make this provision to the victim whose rights sprang from his needs and not from the legal status of the accident that caused those needs.

Thus it was that the violent changes of the Second World War were cushioned by the growth of public provision. This public provision was based on equal treatment of equal needs; the socialist principle of to each according to his needs was therefore adopted; and this entailed progressive taxation – from each according to his ability. The growth of the social services was egalitarian; and to sustain them, the public ownership of the profits of industry and trade was essential. Whether the profits came directly by nationalisation, or indirectly by taxation, was almost immaterial. That, roughly, was the egalitarian case.

As prosperity mounted in the 1950s it was obvious that not only had the breakdown of capitalism which seemed obvious in the early 1930s not occurred; but like a phoenix capitalism had risen from the ashes of the Second World War. Indeed it had risen most dramatically in the defeated nations of Germany, Italy and Japan – literally from the ashes of their destroyed cities and factories. The nature of the society and of the economy that provided this affluence, and extraordinarily high growth rates, was in some respects radically different from earlier periods.

## The affluent society

The economic boom of the 1950s made many people wonder whether modified capitalism had not superseded socialism as the means of achieving prosperity for all

It was a society geared to rapid growth. It was a society with a high prospensity to invest, and it was this high level of investment which explained the full employment levels achieved. Even in the occasional periods of slackening of growth, unemployment rarely rose above 4 per cent in the United States, which was the industrialised country with the highest unemployment levels and which measured its unemployment in such a way that it was always apparently several percentage points above that of the rest of the world. The national income per head rose rapidly and this led to much higher consumption expenditure, especially in the income-elastic areas of consumer durables. For the industrial world outside the United States the 1950s were the years of the car, the television, the washing machine and the refrigerator. There was a dramatic improvement in housing and in the standard of clothing, food and holidays of ordinary people. In the United States, the most prosperous country in the world, many millions of people were sufficiently rich to live in a way hitherto confined to the upper-middle class. Nor was it true that the social services were neglected. Education expenditure rose to 5–7 per cent of the gross national products of most industrial countries. Expenditure on medical services was largely publicly subsidised and reached 4 to 6 per cent of the gross national product (it was lowest in Britain with a comprehensive National Health Service and highest in the United States with a substantial private sector). Social security benefits, especially in France and Germany, rose rapidly, on a basis closely related to earnings. Only in Britain, often regarded as the most left wing of the industrial countries, were social security payments substantially on a flat-rate benefit basis.

The economic underpinning of this affluence was high investment. High investment was determined by high profit rates, which in turn depended on rapidly and steadily rising demand. This depended, in turn, on rapid rises in wages and salaries, which were guaranteed by the full-employment conditions that prevailed, in which employers could usually grant wage rises without pricing their products out of the market. Demand was also kept up by rapidly growing international trade, a growth that was accelerated by the successive measures adopted internationally to reduce or abolish tariffs, quotas and other obstacles to trade, as in the General Agreement on Tariffs and Trade and the tariff-free areas like the European Economic Community. Growing public expenditure, especially on social welfare, and steady expenditure on defence, also kept up demand. In such conditions there was a rising demand, especially for housing, consumer durable goods and services (particularly transport); this led to rising investment, and this high rate of investment led to accelerated technological progress.

The firms that provided this high investment and fast technological progress were unlike the businesses which had built up capitalism. In the first place they were often very big and international, employing many thousands of people and hundreds of millions of dollars of capital in many countries. They did not compete as the neo-classical models said, where many small firms offered the same product, but by offering different products, whose sales they ensured by vigorous advertising and selling effort. Nor were they, like traditional entrepreneurs, concerned mainly with maximising profits. Rather, there was a division of ownership and control. Hundreds of thousands of shareholders were scattered throughout the property-owning classes: many of them held shares indirectly through pension funds, insurance companies and mutual funds, few of them had long-term loyalties to the firms in which they had stock; when the price of shares fell they sold; when the price rose they bought. The management of the companies was in the hands of a professional class of managers, for the greater part salaried, whose loyalty was to the corporation as such. This loyalty was to make the company grow in size and reputation; to market a product of high repute; to serve the public weal by disinterested service; and to be good employers. The net surplus of the country was thus distributed between consumers, workers and stockholders on an equitable basis. The large corporation behaved in fact as a public trustee; and its corporate philosophy was almost indistinguishable from that of the publicly owned body or nationalised industry.

It followed then that modern capitalism was welfare capitalism. The corporations sought steady markets, co-operated with the state and were good employers. They produced sound products and they invested in long-term development and research. In such circumstances to talk of the class war seemed preposterous.

In the 1950s American thinkers pronounced the end of ideologies. Increasingly, as prosperity achieved by high investment, scientific research and technological innovation affected country after country, it would lead to a growing assimilation of ideas and attitudes. The Soviet Union, Europe, America, would all live in a materialist society, using the same artifacts and strangely similar in ideas and outlook. The class war would be over and so would the Cold War. The role

# World government spending in 1961 and 1967

1961
1967

Total Government spending
as a percentage of the
Gross National Product

Education spending as a percentage
of the Gross National Product

Defence spending as a percentage
of the Gross National Product

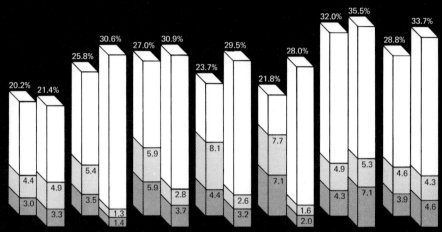

| | Australia | Austria | Belgium | Denmark | Finland | France | West Germany |
|---|---|---|---|---|---|---|---|
| Total 1961 | 20.2% | 25.8% | 27.0% | 23.7% | 21.8% | 32.0% | 28.8% |
| Total 1967 | 21.4% | 30.6% | 30.9% | 29.5% | 28.0% | 35.5% | 33.7% |
| Education 1961 | 4.4 | 5.4 | 5.9 | 8.1 | 7.7 | 4.9 | 4.6 |
| Education 1967 | 4.9 | 1.3 | 2.8 | 2.6 | 7.1 | 5.3 | 4.3 |
| Defence 1961 | 3.0 | 3.5 | 5.9 | 4.4 | 7.1 | 4.3 | 3.9 |
| Defence 1967 | 3.3 | 1.4 | 3.7 | 3.2 | 1.6 / 2.0 | 7.1 | 4.6 |

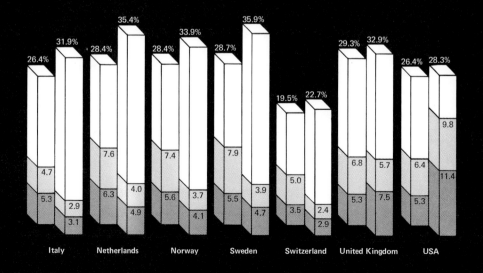

| | Italy | Netherlands | Norway | Sweden | Switzerland | United Kingdom | USA |
|---|---|---|---|---|---|---|---|
| Total 1961 | 26.4% | 28.4% | 28.4% | 28.7% | 19.5% | 29.3% | 26.4% |
| Total 1967 | 31.9% | 35.4% | 33.9% | 35.9% | 22.7% | 32.9% | 28.3% |
| Education 1961 | 4.7 | 7.6 | 7.4 | 7.9 | 5.0 | 6.8 | 6.4 |
| Education 1967 | 2.9 | 4.0 | 3.7 | 3.9 | 2.4 | 5.7 | 9.8 / 11.4 |
| Defence 1961 | 5.3 | 6.3 | 5.6 | 5.5 | 3.5 | 5.3 | 5.3 |
| Defence 1967 | 3.1 | 4.9 | 4.1 | 4.7 | 2.9 | 7.5 | |

of the state would be to provide social services and an economic infrastructure. This might be a public planned economy as in the Soviet Union; or a semi-planned society as in France; but it would in fact be indistinguishable from America.

Two sorts of objection existed to this view. One was the protest of the Third World, that it was excluded from this prosperity, and (along with negroes in the United States) it was prepared to fight for its rights. The other was the challenge to the weight of materialism. Galbraith and others asked what sort of society was being created? It was the creation of useless object after useless object. Consumers' needs were invented by advertising; perfectly usable objects were thrown away because advertising made them obsolete; all spiritual life was atrophied. Meanwhile, the good life depended on public outlays on education and culture, and on preserving the natural and historic environment; and the poor stood outside the gates of the city of affluence. The balance of public and private spending needed to be radically changed.

This became the slogan of social democracy. Socialism returned to its primitive roots. It was against affluence.

# Socialism and the Third World

In the context of the growing Vietnam War, and the profound changes which had taken place since 1945 throughout the formerly colonised areas of the world, socialism tended to be increasingly defined in terms of the needs of the developing nations. These nations found western-style political institutions fitted ill with their circumstances. Many of them became military dictatorships; some, like Algeria, became 'People's Democracies' on the Cuban or Yugoslav model. These regimes required solidarity and intense nationalism, and opposition was met by imprisonment, exile or death. Many of the regimes adopted hostile attitudes to each other; there was the perennial Arab-Israeli conflict, wars in Africa, the Vietnam War, the Indo-Pakistan War, and military confrontations in south-east Asia. All these wars had to be 'contained' for fears of sparking off a Russo-American nuclear war.

Within each country, except Cuba, Algeria and a

handful of others, the military regimes tended to stop short of radical redistribution of the land, nationalisation of domestic industry, and other measures of socialist development, and tended as a result to be dismissed as American puppets by their opponents. There was little doubt that some regimes were installed by the Americans and maintained in office by them – the Dominican Republic and the Saigon Vietnam regimes being instances – but elsewhere it seemed that America had become involved, sometimes against the better judgement of the Department of State, as part of the competition for influence with the Soviet Union or China.

The identification of socialism with poverty, and with hitherto despised racial groups like the Africans, was inevitable. It looked (probably erroneously) as though the prosperity of the West was a reciprocal of the poverty of the East; it could be argued that compensation and blood-money had to be paid. What was less easy to understand was the degree to which socialism was identified with nationalism. People who would have blushed at patriotic fervour at home found patriotic rubbish moving in Lagos, Hanoi or Havana. It was no less rubbish for being black or yellow rubbish, just as tyranny and murder were no less tyranny and murder for being black or yellow.

**Above left:** Nehru helps with a community project of road building, part of an All India programme. While not a socialist by name, he declared at the Aradi Congress of 1955 that India would follow a 'socialistic' pattern of society. The leadership of Third World neutralism was passing to a new breed of Asian socialist.
**Right:** President Nyerere of Tanzania taking part in a 'self help' homebuilding scheme. His 'Arusha declaration' initiated a programme for the establishment of self-reliant village communes

**France**

In France the Social Democrats served in many governments from 1944 to 1958. In 1946 the Communists left the government and de Gaulle resigned. Thereafter the Prime Minister was frequently a socialist. There were four main parties – the Communists, the Socialists, the Catholic Social Democratic Party, and the Radicals. The Communist Party, increasingly intransigent and increasingly in a minority, stood apart from the governmental process, leaving affairs to the other groups in successive coalitions.

These coalition governments achieved a great deal both economically and socially. Some of the economy was nationalised, but the biggest change in the French economy was the introduction of a new concept of central planning. The French *Commissariat au Plan*

French socialist poster of 1946 claiming credit for the partial nationalisation of industry by the postwar coalition government. The SFIO promoted itself as an alternative to communism on the one

dès 1919
le PARTI SOCIALISTE S.F.I.O. réclame la nationalisation des
**GRANDS TRUSTS**

BANQUES
CREDIT
*GRANDS TRUSTS*
PETROLE
ASSURANC

*SOCIALISATION!*

was established at the heart of government, its task
being mainly to plan physical investment in the public
sector and by a process of consultation and encourage-
ment to plan investment in the private sector as well.
The result was a significant advance in the rate of
economic growth and the redevelopment of France.

The weakness of the economy was the rate of
domestic inflation, which was related to weakness in the
external balance. The inflation was, in one respect, a
strength, because under inflation the level of profit
continually grows and this encourages investment. It
led, however, to a sense of threat and weakness, to
which the chronic instability of the regime contributed.
The external balance was cushioned by American aid,
through the European Recovery Program, and by frequent devaluations. France thus had rapid economic
growth and a substantial social reform programme,
especially in education, where from the point of view
of numbers, France led Europe.

The weakness of the regime was political. It was
unable to control wage demands and unable to stop
inflation. Its foreign policy was necessarily tied to a
desire to restore the French position in the world but
this desire was inhibited by the weakness of the balance
of payments. France entered the North Atlantic Alliance. It also took a leading part in the movement
which culminated in the Treaty of Rome and the establishment of the European Economic Community.

French socialism was therefore interpreted as economic growth, social reform and European unity, an
interpretation largely due to the influence of the
moderate Catholic reformers, similar to those in office
in Germany and Italy. The Common Market, which
was the institutional form taken by the movement for
European unity, was basically a liberal Catholic
conception.

The opposition to this concept was threefold. The
Communist Party, which had the traditional support
of a number of working-class people, was a close follower of the Moscow line and, as the French government allied itself firmly with the North Atlantic group,
this meant that the Communist party was profoundly
opposed to the regime. In this they were joined by the
Gaullists, who were intensely nationalist and who

completely rejected the concept of a North American and a European world in which individual nationalist loyalties would be subsumed into a wider internationalism. This nationalism was accentuated by the inability of the Fourth Republic governments to settle the French colonial problem. In the first place there was the war in Vietnam, leading to the humiliating defeat and withdrawal of 1954. This blow was bad enough but the Algerian situation was worse.

Algeria was not a colony. Like Ireland under the Union with Great Britain, it was constitutionally an integral part of France and many Algerians were French or of French descent. The simple solution of withdrawing from Algeria seemed to involve betraying compatriots, as well as abandoning the 'civilising mission' of France – the leaders of Algeria were all products of high French culture.

Algeria divided France. The army and the Gaullists were determined not to leave, but to subdue the nationalists; the communists and the left were determined to leave Algeria; the governments vacillated. The socialists, on the whole, sided with the army. The philosophical debate was of great significance.

On the one side the Marxists and democratic socialists, deeply concerned about colonialism, regarded the Fourth Republic as a contemptible engine of bourgeois repression. The most distinguished French thinkers – Sartre, for example – who were ex-Marxists, or neo-Marxists, found Algeria the test of their commitment to humane values and to the support of revolutionary forces. On the other side, the army and the gaullist socialists developed a concept of radical nationalism, which would use the paternal strength of the army to regenerate France and to purify its civilisation. No French thinker of any distinction supported the moderate social policy and parliamentary institutions of the Fourth Republic.

The Republic collapsed in 1958 and de Gaulle assumed power, establishing a familiar type of plebiscitary presidency, such as Napoleon III had maintained. By a series of moves of political genius, worthy of Gladstone or Parnell, Roosevelt or Bismarck, he withdrew from Algeria. Gradually, too, he extricated himself from the growing internationalism of European policy. He also managed to reverse the adverse balance of payments and to attract considerable quantities of gold to France.

Thus, by the mid-1960s, de Gaulle had consolidated the economic and social achievements of the Fourth Republic, he had ended the colonial problem, and he had achieved an independent foreign policy. To a considerable degree political activity had stopped in France. Parliament was far less important than it had been since it lacked the effective power to make or break governments. The socialist movement, split by Algeria, had to a considerable degree become Gaullist. Opposition to the regime by socialists was sporadic and ineffective, and was to remain so through the student uprising of May 1968, and after the resignation

# Pragmatism and the new frontiers

British socialism passed through successive crises in the 1950s. There is no doubt that despite Labour's striking achievements in social policy, it was identified in the public mind with austerity and rationing. Before 1955, however, the Conservatives restored a great deal of the free market and consumption levels rose, while there was no reduction in social benefits nor any rise in unemployment. The fears that the Conservatives would dismantle the welfare state and introduce mass unemployment were allayed and in 1955 they won the general election with a big majority. This electoral defeat accelerated the process of the Labour Party's rethinking of strategy, policies and philosophy.

Hugh Gaitskell succeeded Attlee as Labour leader after the 1955 election. His first major political act was a confrontation with the Conservatives over the Anglo-French-Israeli invasion of Suez. During the period leading up to the invasion, and during the invasion, the Labour Party for the most part attacked the government violently. For once, the Labour Party was almost united in its support of two tried policies – anti-colonialism and backing for the United Nations – without regard to the narrow interests of the country. Thus Gaitskell opened his period as leader with strong and wide support. The exception was an important one – the majority of working-class voters supported the invasion. Their sense of patriotism and nationalism was outraged by the internationalism of the Labour leadership. This was to be important in the 1959 election.

During the period from 1955 a major debate took place about the future of socialism. Up to 1959 this debate was concerned with the policy of the impending Labour government which it was expected would be

## Socialism and Pragmatism in Britain and Europe

**Opposite:** 1956 cartoon of the Suez Crisis, showing Conservative Prime Minister Anthony Eden confronted with the leader of the 'shadow' Labour opposition Hugh Gaitskell: 'funny, I thought my shadow was always behind me'. The Labour Party was violently opposed to the invasion of Suez

elected in 1959. After the defeat of the Labour Party
in that election, the debate was more ferocious because
what now seemed to be in question was whether or not
the Labour Party would survive at all.

The debate was about three things. The first was
whether or not the economic problem had fundamentally been solved. The great growth of affluence in
North America and Western Europe had eroded many
of the socialist positions. The Keynesian solution to
the question of unemployment seemed to have been
successful and had been followed by economic growth
in a process that was continuous and irreversible.
There was little point in socialism as such if its aim
was to overthrow the system in order to achieve what
the system was already doing. Gaitskell, as an economist, was concerned to improve economic management and he found it less successful in Britain than
elsewhere; but in essence his criticisms were criticisms
of detail. Despite casual references to international
monetary problems, neither he nor his colleagues foresaw the monetary crises of the later 1960s.

Because the economic problem was solved (and those
who denied this did so for visceral rather than intellectual reasons) nationalisation became irrelevant. There
might be particular arguments for particular cases but,
in general, nationalisation would not accelerate economic growth. Nationalisation and economic controls
had been and remained extremely unpopular. Why
saddle the Labour Party with an ideological commitment to a goal whose interest was purely sentimental?
This became an issue of great significance – especially
à propos of steel – but Gaitskell's position was, broadly
speaking, adopted.

Assuming steady economic growth, socialism became a doctrine about three things. The first was the
division of the spoils. A proportion of the population
seemed to be missed out by economic growth. It was
necessary to build up the social services to eliminate
poverty. This would lead to a far more egalitarian
society. The thesis was that technical and economic
progress had outdistanced social change – that a dynamic
economy was held back by an outmoded social structure. The social services were to be lavishly endowed
with the fruits of economic growth and the whole

policy rested on the assumption that the latter would continue and accelerate.

The second pillar of socialist doctrine was the quality of life. Society had to be made more equal and more just but it also had to be made more liberal and more beautiful. The reform of the penal system, the removal of penalties for homosexuality, the legalisation of abortion, the removal of puritan restrictions of all kinds, were some aspects of liberalism. Another aspect was an attempt to strengthen democratic institutions, in politics, in industry and in society.

The third platform of revisionist socialism was an attempt to redress the balance of the world by helping the developing nations, both through aid and through institutions in international trade, which would raise the prices of primary products.

The attacks on this reform movement came from those who held that the capitalist economy was bound to run into crisis; that the affluent society was debasing the culture and leading to increased alienation of the workers from the dominant social values; and that the world crisis, shown in the Third World, would bring down the institutions both of the West and of Russia, which were designed to entrench a powerful bureaucratic class.

Gaitskell died and his former opponent Wilson was elected leader of the Labour Party. In 1964 Labour won a narrow electoral victory and in 1966 a much larger majority. In the event it followed Gaitskell's policy, enlarging the social services and introducing or supporting a great deal of liberal legislation.

But two major problems affected it. The first was

The Labour cabinet of 1966 with the Prime Minister Harold Wilson. On the extreme left is the influential writer and thinker Richard Crossman, to the Prime Minister's left are Dennis Healey and Roy Jenkins, and at the extreme right is Anthony Wedgwood Benn, the advocate of technological innovations

Cartoon by Gerald
Scarfe from 1962.
Harold Wilson's
attempt to enforce an
incomes policy was
one of the main causes
of his electoral
defeat in 1970

that the economy got increasingly out of control,
mainly because of the growing international monetary
crisis, which centred on Britain and inhibited any
policies that appeared to threaten the balance of payments. The repeated crises in the external balance,
which led to devaluation and then to further difficulties, also led to a low rate of economic growth – which
removed the basis of the Gaitskellite programme of
financing the growing social services from the fruits
of economic development. It also destroyed much of
the credibility of the government, especially with the
working people, who were subjected to constantly

increasing prices, rising tax rates and wage control.

The crises also inhibited foreign policy. Wilson's government was a supporter of the United States war in Vietnam; its independent foreign policy crashed on to the rocks of the monetary questions; it was unable to help the Third World.

By the late 1960s, the question was no longer what was the content of revised socialism. It appeared that revisionist socialism had died. It had been replaced by nationalist scientific-militarism, which was in control of many countries and which would determine the future, if any, of the world.

The election of J. F. Kennedy in 1960, by a hairs-breadth, marked an apparently radical change in the style of American government. It was in fact symptomatic of changes that occurred in the late 1950s, and early 1960s throughout the industrialised world.

## Kennedy and the New Frontier

The significance of Kennedy for democratic socialism lay more in his rhetoric than in his actions. He adopted wholeheartedly the view that the affluent society had overcome the economic problems that had beset earlier societies. By accelerating public expenditure he raised the United States growth rate; by accelerating the growth rate, the United States became more affluent than ever before. The Administration devised programmes for an attack on poverty. Kennedy's concern was for the poor – for improving their housing, their environment, their health, their education and their incomes. Thus there were Poverty Programs,

President Kennedy defending medical care for the aged at a meeting of the National Council of Senior Citizens in New York

1961. 'I tell yer, the guy's a dangerous socialist'. British cartoon on the American reaction to President Kennedy's welfare programme

Urban Programs, Health-Care Programs, and Education Programs. Many of these were enacted only after Kennedy's assassination in Dallas, Texas, in 1963, and pushed through by his successor Lyndon B. Johnson, in his Great Society Program, but in essence the diagnosis of the situation was the one expounded by the men and women brought to Washington by Kennedy in what was known as the New Frontier.

This New Frontier was a rhetorical device for making the discoveries – or alleged discoveries – of the social sciences palatable. In the first place, it was now known that social problems appeared in clusters; that social disadvantages were cumulative; to tackle any one in isolation was to attack a symptom for increasingly, the roots of inequality were to be seen in the whole environment of the disadvantaged. It would not be enough to raise material standards only – though, politically and economically that would be a heroic enough task – but the deeper sources of motivation for achievement had to be tapped. This implied a coordinated programme of reform – socio-psychological action of a kind that had never been attempted before and about which little was known even in theory – in order to achieve a radical transformation of society.

It was this attitude of the New Frontier that was enshrined in Crosland's dictum that equality of opportunity was not enough; the conditions had to be created which gave equality in the opportunity to acquire ability. It seemed as though ability was more an acquired rather than an inherited characteristic; and whatever the 'scientific' truth about 'ability' – which was certainly not an inherited characteristic like the colour of the eyes but a conglomerate of attitudes and talents – for public policy purposes it was a respectable assumption that the environment could be to some degree controlled whereas inheritance could not be. The attack on the deprived environment, through a series of laws and the voting of substantial sums of money, was, therefore, the domestic policy of the New Frontier.

It involved, first, legislation about racial equality. The Supreme Court had ruled for some years that racial equality was guaranteed by the Constitution; the legislation proposed by the New Frontier (especially about voter registration) was designed to implement this guarantee. But racial equality was not merely a matter of formal equality of voting rights. It was necessary to have social equality if political equality were to be meaningful. Social inequality in the United States rested most strongly on the historic division between slave and free, and it would take profound efforts to overcome these inherited disadvantages.

In America, in essence, domestic policy of this sort had been predominantly a matter for the states, and the complexity of arranging for Federal intervention was one of the reasons for the slowness of the programme. It was also undertaken within a framework of constitutional law which both inhibited some action (the Federal government, for example, could not directly provide schools) and created situations with which the Federal government had to deal. The Supreme Court accelerated the process of civil rights for Negroes by a series of judgements; legislation followed to enforce these judgements.

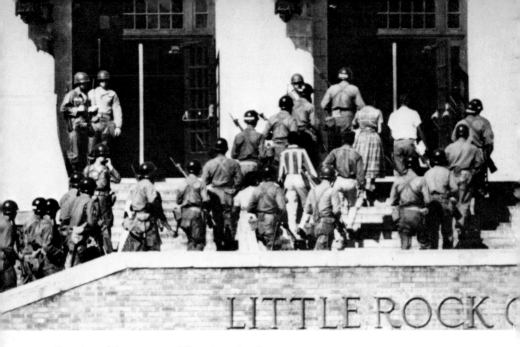

LITTLE ROCK (

Thus by the later 1960s American society was a complex of private and public initiatives. The majority – the great majority – of the population was richer than people in other countries, except Canada, Sweden and Switzerland. Educational outlays were greater than elsewhere and a higher proportion of young people was at school and college than elsewhere in the world. Social security was, in some respects, better than in Britain. It is true that health care was expensive and there was no comprehensive system of medical provision or insurance payments; yet this was due less to some innate capitalist weakness than to the extraordinary power of the American Medical Association in holding the community to ransom – a power that a complex constitution enhanced (as it enhanced the power of all pressure groups). Racial inequality was obvious; yet the Negroes (except in some of the southern states) were not necessarily as relatively deprived as the urban poor of some other advanced countries or as the depressed rural minorities in the Soviet Union. Above all, representative political institutions worked in a constitutional framework. To strike a balance with the Soviet Union, it would be easy to say that all but the very poorest Americans were better off than the Russians, that education was better but the health service worse, but that above all the Americans had freedom of expression and democratic institutions.

Yet the Great Society collapsed politically, to be followed by Nixon's election in 1968. The first reason was the war in Vietnam. Successive American Presidents, but especially Kennedy and Johnson, became involved in a holding operation in Vietnam which in effect meant supporting a corrupt regime in the south against a communist regime in the north. Involvement in a civil war is always unwise; in this case it was catastrophic since it led to allegations that the 'true face' of American capitalism was revealed in Vietnam.

The next reason was black militancy. It has been repeatedly shown that when a depressed group begins to make economic, political or social gains it will become more militant. So it was with black Americans. This militancy, concentrated in the northern cities, attracted support from young radicals, already alienated from the Great Society by the Vietnam War, and drove many respectable people in the opposite direction, escecially when it took the specific form of campus revolts, sit-ins and violence in the universities.

Thirdly, the Great Society's full employment policies added to America's unfavourable balance of payments situation, which jeopardised her position in the world monetary system and led to continuous price and wage rises which revived fears of a steady inflation. This in itself represented a threat to middle-class Americans, which redoubled their dislike of the Democrats.

To be radical in America, therefore, meant to be identified with the anti-Vietnam cause, to sympathise with Cuba, to sympathise with the Negroes, and to regard these three problems as systematically connected – the responsibility of capitalism. More important, the collapse of cultural values – the impoverishment of American education, the cheapjack nature of American society – was regarded as being due to the same cause. The affluent society, far from being the Great Society, struck radicals as being rotten to the core. But, it has to be said, this diagnosis was an impressionistic one; and there was no coherent alternative, since Marxism (except possibly in the romantic revolutionary Cuban case) had proved to be equally bankrupt.

# The proportion of Socialist
# and Social Democratic governments
# 1920-70

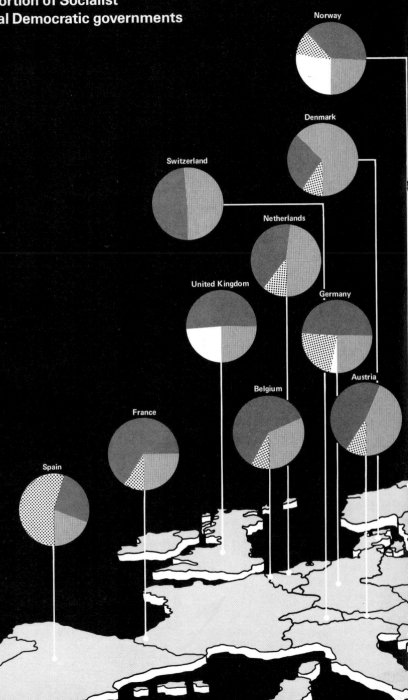

Italy

Hungary

Czechoslovakia

Sweden

Finland

New Zealand

Poland

Australia
(Federal Government)

☐ Socialist or social democratic governments

▦ Social democrats in coalition or minority governments

▦ Other democratic parties in power

▨ No democracy: totalitarian regimes, fascist
or communist

# Democratic Socialism

1950 cartoon of the British Labour Party: 'the man who mention-ed Marx at a socialist gathering'. Social democracy had travel-led far from its starting point. (The man is Aneurin Bevan who was, until his death, the chief representative of the left-wing of the Labour Party)

Democratic socialism was committed to constitutional action and not to revolution. Like Parnell's Irish Party, it had to achieve its aim through parliamentary insti-tutions. This involved compromises. At what point the compromises involved betrayal was the perennial question. In part it depended on the nature of the constitution and of the attacks on it. Were imperial Germany, fascist Italy or Gaullist France intolerable regimes that had to be violently overthrown? Or could they be reformed from within? If the attacks on the regime came from communists, or anarchists, or fascists, determined to establish a tyranny, should not a democratic socialist defend institutions that, how-ever imperfect, guaranteed some sort of public order, some freedom from arbitrary arrest, some freedom from terror, and had some hope of reform? The answer depended partly on the degree of horror that was evoked by the attacks; John Dillon, the last leader of the Irish Parliamentary Party, said after the Irish Civil War that he would almost have preferred to continue the Union with Great Britain than live under the nationalist terror. A democratic socialist has often been in this position. He sees a choice between evils; he does not see a Utopia.

To be a democrat, therefore, is to regard the pos-sibility of revolution as something to be avoided at

almost all costs. To be a social democrat is, however,
to hold that this constitutional parliamentary process
can be used for social engineering to make society more
rational. Rationality – and this is a huge claim – would,
it is held, lead to a more desirable, a softer, more prosperous, more equal and more just society. Rationality
involved the understanding of society. Social democracy, therefore, is the application through social
engineering of the findings of the social sciences.

Democratic socialists, therefore, in contrast to the
Marxists (who had a revealed doctrine) had the pragmatic, empirical application of transitory findings as
the body of their approach. If, as often happened, the
social sciences were wrong, or were wrongly interpreted, democratic socialism failed its own tests. In any
event, too, the world has often, perhaps usually, preferred irrationality; in olden times it preferred religion
and now it prefers nationalism.

The findings of economics on the causes of unemployment and economic growth drove democratic
socialists to seek to use the power of the state to create
employment and to hasten innovation by promoting
investment. The process of economic policy-making
involved the greater use of state power; but not
necessarily its use in a direction of greater equality
and social reform. The process of wage control, for

The Cold War forced
social democrats to
side with the United
States against the
Soviet Union. British
cartoon of Prime
Minister Harold
Wilson: 'We have
established our special
relationship with the
United States'

example, which is an integral part of the programme for economic growth, necessarily involves a redistribution of the national product away from the wage-earning class. The building up of investment almost necessarily involves an increase in the level of profits. It does not necessarily follow, therefore, that economics will lead to socialism.

Nor does it follow that sociology will. The discovery of the extremely deep roots of inequality entails the possibility of extremely radical measures to uproot inequality – including the abolition of the family. Are democratic socialists prepared to accept a society of social isolates? Obviously not. Yet, to retain an organic society would involve the acceptance of inequality and of apparent irrationalities which were contrary to socialist principles.

In the world context, then, democratic socialism shows itself as a cautious, pragmatic series of policies formulated within a constitutional political framework. This doctrine is profoundly antipathetic to nationalism, and to all mass movements that seem to be irrational and destructively revolutionary, or blindly reactionary. Thus, in the last analysis, democratic socialists are bound to be pro-American and hostile to the Soviet Union though their sentiments may be more anti-American (because America is perceived as the heart of the capitalist world) and pro-Russian (because Russia is perceived as a lapsed socialist society). In a world deeply divided between militaristic regimes of various kinds linked by military agreements, democratic socialists – save in small neutral countries like Sweden – are bound to be committed to the foreign policy objectives of the group of nations to which their own country is allied, for to be radical with respect to that policy would mean – in effect – to change sides.

This is even true in the Third World. Not only have socialists found it very hard to come to terms with militarism – so that over half the developing nations had military regimes – but the existence of a struggle between super-powers has meant that neutralism was almost bound to dissolve into support for one side or another.

Democratic socialism presumes an ordered society; if that ordered society is in a state of military readiness,

The German SPD leader Willi Brandt, who became the first post-war socialist Chancellor of West Germany

Cartoon of the British Trade Union Movement, 1969. The conservatism of the trade unions has proved a major stumbling block to socialist governments in Britain

militarism will always be the dominant of the two forces.

Another element which democratic socialism has found it increasingly difficult to cope with is trade unionism. Democratic socialism, like any socialism, is linked with a concept of the working class as the vanguard of the struggle for a better social order. Yet the trade unions, deeply sunk in bureaucratic lethargy, have rarely been seen as such except by their most addled bourgeois admirers. In the modern, post-capitalist world the trade unions are part of the bureaucratic power structure. To be radical is to be against them. A rational incomes policy requires their powers – like those of other oligopoly groups – to be controlled by the state in 'the public interest'. Yet the democratic socialist movement depends for its financial and organisational strength on the trade unions. Thus democratic socialism is bound to compromise its radicalism with reality; its concern with the future is affected by its history as a class-party.

This inability to deal with two powerful interests – militarism and trade unionism – immediately raises the conflict between the ideals of equality and social justice and the demands of pragmatism. Harold Wilson was just the latest of a long series of social democratic leaders who were accused of selling their principles for pragmatic advantages – keeping office for the sake of keeping office.

The implementation of socialist principles is handicapped by the vagueness of the principles and by the fact that to implement social change requires a complex strategy of social engineering. This has to be superimposed on a state machine that is an on-going concern; and it has to be done within the limits of political possibility. In such a situation, it might seem that the surprising thing is not how little is done, but how

## Trade Union Membership in some major West European countries between 1914 and 1966

|  | 1913/14 | 1935/36 | 1965/66 |
|---|---|---|---|
| Denmark | 132 | 381 | 978 |
| France | 1,064 | 5,000 | 3,002 (Excluding Communists) |
| Germany | 5,590 | Not Free | 7,717 |
| Italy | 321 | Not Free | 3,002 |
| Norway | 76 | 224 | 575 |
| Sweden | 111 | 701 | 2,277 |
| United Kingdom | 2,200 | 5,295 | 8,878 (1,000,000 not in TUC) |

much. A practical conviction that decency, moderation and freedom are not only essential to the good life, but can be achieved, is almost heroic in a century that has seen such horrors committed in the name of great ideals. Social democrats dislike the label of 'idealist' for this reason. That their ideals are those that all civilised people must hold if they are honest with themselves is, however, their great strength.

Social democracy throughout its history has been handicapped by its preference for pragmatism over ideology. Conservative Party election poster from 1970

# Remember Labour's broken promises

# Bibliography

This book is in a series which includes *Capitalism, Communism* and *Fascism*, all of which suggest books that are essential for an understanding of the historical and intellectual climate of democratic socialism. The reader should study the socialist classics – Proudhon, Marx, Engels – which are referred to in other and fuller bibliographies. The following secondary works will be found useful. The list is pruned drastically from a very much longer list of works consulted; this will appear in a further volume, shortly to be published, called *Inequality*.

First is G. D. H. Cole's *A History of Socialist Thought,* 5 volumes, London 1953–1960, which is diffuse but essential reading.

There are a number of important historical works – some of the most interesting of relatively recent date are:

| | |
|---|---|
| M. Beer | *A History of British Socialism,* London, 1948. |
| Alexander Gray | *The Socialist Tradition,* London, 1946. |
| P. Gay | *The Dilemma of Democratic Socialism,* New York, 1952. |
| D. Ligou | *Histoire du Socialisme en France, 1871–1961,* Paris, 1962. |
| Edouard Dolléan | *Histoire du Mouvement Ouvrier,* Vols. 2 and 3, Paris, 1939–1953. |

J. D. Caute, *The Left in Europe* (1966), is a useful panoramic study from a neo-Marxist standpoint. H. Pelling, *A Short History of the Labour Party* (1961), gives a clear account of the development of the Labour Party. Hugh Thomas, *The Spanish Civil War* (1961), describes the failure of all moderate movements, including social democracy, in Spain. E. J. Hobsbawm's *Industry and Empire* (1968), is especially helpful.

J. A. Schumpeter's *Capitalism, Socialism and Democracy* (2nd edition, 1947) remains in many ways the most stimulating and worthwhile book on the subject. It is full of intelligence, scholarship and wit. Works which partly derive from it, like *Modern Capitalism* by Andrew Shonfield (1965), and J. K. Galbraith's *The Affluent Society* (1958), are more up-to-date but less incisive. George Lichtheim's *A Short History of Socialism* (1970) is lucid and well worth study.

Some important statements on modern democratic socialism are C. A. R. Crosland, *The Future of Socialism* (1956), Evan Durbin, *The Politics of Democratic Socialism* (1940), and Arthur Lewis, *The Principles of Economic Planning* (1949).

John Strachey in his last books, *Contemporary Capitalism* (1956), and *The End of Empire* (1959), made important contributions to the theory of modern social democracy.

Gunnar Myrdal, especially in *Value in Social Theory* (1958), attacks the notion of 'free' social services, and thus provides a basis for the refusal to accept the market, or some other self-regulating mechanism, as a basis of the social order.

Joan Robinson's *An Essay on Marxian Economics* (1942) remains a standard work on Marxist economics, studied from a social democratic standpoint. Thomas Balogh's *The Economics of Poverty* (1966) is also relevant. For a criticism of neo-classical economics Nicholas Kaldor's *Essays on Value and Distribution* (1960) is especially helpful. Piero Sraffa's *Production of Commodities by Means of Commodities* (1960), has been called the most important economics book of the century; in this context its importance lies in its profound reinterpretation of classical economics. Robin Marris's *The Economic Theory of 'Managerial' Capitalism* (1964) will repay study.

Among sociological works that are relevant, R. H. Tawney's *Equality* (1931), is, of course, of central importance as is T. H. Marshall, *Citizenship and Social Class*, 1950. R. H. S. Crossmann (ed.) *The God That Failed*, (1950), and Arthur Koestler in *The Yogi and the Commissar* (1945) are works that explain the background to a non-Marxist alternative to Marx's view of society, based on disillusionment with Stalinist Marxist régimes.

In recent German publications there is no better historical work than Carl Schorske's *German Social Democracy 1905–1917* (1955). For the later period there is no good standard work in English.

J. L. Talmon's *The Origins of Totalitarian Democracy* (1952), is an important work for the pluralistic basis of social democracy. It relies in part on C. R. Popper's *The Open Society and Its Enemies* (2 volumes, 4th edition, 1962). E. M. Forster, *Two Cheers for Democracy* (1951), expresses the moderate civilised tone in which politics ought to be conducted, as does A. J. P. Taylor in *English History 1914–45*, (1965). George Lichtheim in his *Marxism* (1961) takes a profoundly depressing view both of social democracy and of Marxism, which is a useful corrective to the view presented here.

Sir Isaiah Berlin in *Four Essays on Liberty*, (1969), offers an interpretation of freedom in a democratic social order which most nearly accords with the view presented here.

# Index